TRANSITION:
Ashes Emanating Beauty

presented by:

Precious Brown

KILGORE PUBLISHING
Flint Michigan
Since 2015

Transition 2: Ashes Emanating Beauty
Copyright © 2017 by Precious Brown

All rights are reserved. Except as permitted under the U.S. Copyright Act of 1976, no part of the publication may be reproduced, distributed or transmitted in any form or by any means, or stored in a database or retrieval system without the prior written permission of the publisher.

All references or direct quotes of scriptures were obtained from various versions of the King James Bible.

This book is available in volume for qualifying organizations. Please contact the presenter to inquire. info@penamasterpiece.com.

For more information about this book, coaching, or speaking engagements please visit www.penamasterpiece.com or email info@penamasterpiece.com.

ISBN 978-0-9961347-7-4
For Worldwide Distribution
Printed in the U.S.A

Table Contents

Forward by Rasheena M. Perry, B.Th, M.Div.

Journey to Celibacy.................................... 1
Precious S. Brown

Permission Granted ………...………………... 7
Tyree L. Groves

Living A Shade of Gray……...……...…………… 18
Valencia Griffin-Wallace

Trapped in the Jewelry Box …………………….. 30
Tasheikya Hunter

Survival Game…………………. ……………….. 50
Shawonia Thomas

Broken Chains………….. ………………….…… 60
Evelyn R. Donelson, M.Ed

Pain to Purpose..……... ……………………..….... 87
Precious S. Brown

Meet the Authors ……………………………….… 100

Forward

The word ashes often recall thoughts of a fire, a death by cremation or the remains of something that has been destroyed. For most, it indicates that the very presence of life; the existence of someone or something is completely over. With that comes sadness, a period of mourning and an emptiness that cannot be refilled. Seemingly, the ashes are just a symbol; a remembrance that may hold sentimental value in one's heart, yet, they appear void of life or power because all we see and feel is the residue that remains. Blinded by our pain and dark memories of the flames; we forget that there's still beauty emanating from the ashes. Women all over the world no matter our race, color or creed, can identify a point and time in our lives when we were left with nothing but the ashes. Death, divorce, sexual abuse, domestic violence, sickness and other life-altering events are all traumatic experiences that potentially disrupted and stagnated our lives. Leaving us buried under the ashes.

Let's use ourselves as a metaphor for the ashes. Sometimes we cleaned ourselves up and made our ashes look nice and pretty, all the while knowing that we were broken down, beat up, and still slowly burning away. Other times we wallowed in them, afraid to stop mourning our loss or recovering from our trauma. We haphazardly spread them all over, until our marriages, children, friends, careers, dreams and more were covered in ashes too! In their real form, people keep them in a pretty Urn, while others scatter them in oceans or even sweep them up as trash. Nevertheless, when mentioned there generally referred to as "ashes."

In Transition: Ashes Emanating Beauty, Author, Wordsmith, Transition Engineer, and Power Coach for women - Precious Brown, has produced an abstract collective of real life stories that bring the subtitle "Ashes Emanating Beauty" to life. In a subtle, yet intriguing way the subtitle appears to be a type of hypothetical anomaly, when, in essence, it is indeed a confirmation of the scripture being brought into existence as they share true stories and life lessons of how they allowed the beauty to develop out of what was once mere ashes.

As it is written in the King James Version of the Bible, Isaiah 61:3 says, "*To appoint unto them that mourn in Zion, to give unto them beauty for ashes, the oil of joy for mourning, the garment of praise for the spirit of heaviness; that they might be called trees of righteousness, the planting of the LORD, that he might be glorified.*"

The word emanating means to flow out; to come forth; to proceed. Precious Brown has set a precedent in her Transition Series that encourages women to tap into their spiritual and inner strength to make their Transition. None of them are one in the same; yet they are all in the position of giving birth, to new life as the ashes are cleared to make way for the beauty of their true selves as they emerge into the Masterpiece they were created to be.

Rasheena M. Perry, B.Th, M.Div

Journey to Celibacy

In a perfect world celibacy is encouraged throughout adolescence up to marriage. The goal was to remain pure and untouched by a man/woman until your wedding night. I wish someone had told me. Unfortunately, when I was growing up it wasn't something we discussed in our family. For years, I had been molested. I didn't know it was wrong. I didn't think of it as having sex. Honestly, I wasn't old enough to know what it was. What I did know is it made me tingle all over. At first I felt something was wrong but the more it happened, with different people, I began to look forward to it. I thought it was normal. I thought that was how people who loved you treated you. At least that's what they told me.

Around the age of 10 my life changed. I was not around some of the same people anymore. I began to have a normal, stable life and the molestation ended. I suppressed the feelings and thoughts. I thought it was better to not tell anybody. I kept all the secrets to myself. I felt safe and I was a happy child and I didn't want that to change. I didn't understand what the shift was or why it happened but I was learning to enjoy doing kid stuff. Playing with my friends, playing sports, jump rope, etcetera. I didn't think much of this new-found happiness. I didn't question it because I liked the space I was in. I enjoyed laughing and having structure in my life again.

Then I arrived in the eighth grade and I noticed boys. Not just seeing them, but really liking them. They were cute (some of them anyway). I noticed those old feelings were coming back stronger. Those same feelings I had when I was younger. I decided to talk to someone about it. Who better than my mom right? In my mind, all moms had this talk with their kids. The sex talk with my mother went like this:

"Mom, can you tell me about sex?"

"Do you know what you are doing?" she said.

"NO!" I said with a scrunched face.

"Then don't do it" she said as she continued to wash the dishes.

That was the entire conversation. It helped me keep my legs closed until I was 15. Little did I know, once the lid was lifted from my deep dark secret sex box it would be a whirlwind of pain to get the top closed again.

At the time, I had a boyfriend who I thought I was in love with. It never dawned on me that I had no clue what love was. I didn't know that sex was all a game to boys at that age. After having my first "real" sexual encounter I was devastated! I realized I had done this before! Yuck! Disgust settled in. All the memories and pain came flooding back and I couldn't stop it. I tried to cope as best I could without telling anyone but my insides were out of control. Soon after that encounter I found out he was interested in someone else.

"How could he", I thought! It wasn't a few months later I was being dumped on my front porch through the screen door. From that instant I vowed no one else would have the opportunity to hurt me again. I would not be anyone else's victim; period!

As hard as I tried the memories would not stop. The feelings of inadequacy and worthlessness became all too familiar. I began to cope with smoking weed and drinking on occasion. But once I was sober everything was the same. I did not know how to break the cycle but what I did know; sex was my weapon and I could use it whenever I wanted. It made me feel as if I were in control. When I said "No", the begging ensued. When I said "Yes" I could get anything I wanted. I began to manipulate men for time, material things and money. The tables had turned and I was the game master. It was great and I felt I was winning; How naïve was that?

Transition: Ashes Emanating Beauty

Sex became the foundation of EVERY relationship I had going forward. I began to run through guys like changing clothes. It didn't matter who they were. Sometimes I didn't even know their names. As the years went on I would get hurt by a guy and the next one would pay for it. The more hurt seemed to come my way by men, the more I self-medicated. The cycle was getting out of control, but I had no way to stop it; nor did I want to.

By age 20 there was another shift happening but I wasn't sure what it was. I was suspicious of it but I was willing to try it. A monogamous relationship was on the horizon. This would be a first for me. I never realized, until now, that relationship was also founded with sex. The relationship lasted 17 years ending in divorce.

It was second nature for me to return to my old ways almost immediately. I was on the hunt. The game had changed a lot since the last time I played but I was willing to learn the rules. I remember thinking "I've been out of this game a long time; but let the good times roll!" Boy, was I wrong. It was not fun at all. I still felt empty. "What is this feeling? Why can't I fill this void?" I asked myself. As time went on I began to spend more time alone. I was facing my past hurts. Learning to forgive those that hurt me as a child. Reflecting on my actions up to that time in my life and how they effected my children. I was in the process of a major change.

Not long after my first divorce I was dating again. I met a man that I thought was totally different than any man I had encountered. We dated off and on for about six years before deciding to get married. At one point, we abstained from sex. I was testing my personal theory about me and sex based relationships. Soon after the nuptials the love affair went south. The marriage lasted a little less than eight months and I was back to the drawing board.

During the breakup, I decided to really do some soul searching as it related to men and sex. I was very conscience of my behavior so I would not do the same thing that I had always done. I decided I wanted different results for my next relationship. I was committed to serving God and I knew I wanted to save my body for the husband God created for me. This was the first time in my life I ever thought about saving myself sexually.

The journey has now been three years and I never have been more content, focused and balanced. I have learned a lot about me and my body. I have risen above excuses on why I need to have sex and the void I tried to fill for over 30 years is now completely healed. This journey has taught me more about my emotions and expectations than anything else. For those of you that may be silently headed down this sex slave road I encourage you to be honest with yourself and answer these questions:

1. Do you feel whole without a sexual partner?
2. What is the longest you have abstained from sex?
3. How do you feel if you are not sexually active?
4. Is my relationship based on sex?
5. How would I feel if I stopped having sex right now?

You always have a chance to change your life by simply changing your actions.

Precious S. Brown

Permission Granted

Grow through what you go through – Unknown

Remember, nothing in this world can be done to you, without permission.

I've stared in the mirror as a young girl daydreaming that I was casting out demons in Jesus' name, understanding that **for we wrestle not against flesh and blood, but against principalities, against powers, against the rulers of the darkness of this world, against spiritual wickedness in high places.** I believe whole-heartedly when Jesus said **"if I bind it on earth, He'll bind it in Heaven; if I loose it on earth, He'll loose it in Heaven, and if I just ask in His name, it shall be done.**

*So, w*hen it comes to the enemy, I will not be fooled, tricked or bamboozled. When the day finally came, I boldly looked him in his face, and let him know, that I knew who he was. He smiled at me, we danced the evening away and I invited him in for a nightcap.

He had been around before, trying to tempt me and sway me into his world, this time was different; he watched and he waited. I had been under surveillance for about seven months before he approached me this time. I was raised to see the enemy for who he was. I was bred to defeat him at all cost and to not let him in. Once he is

Transition: Ashes Emanating Beauty

allowed in, it is hard to get him out. And if you do get him out and allow him to return, he tends to have a stronger hold on you than he had before. He comes to the newly cleaned house with seven more demons stronger than he.

Then it goes and takes with it seven other spirits more wicked than itself, and they go in and live there. And the final condition of that person is worse than the first. That is how it will be with this wicked generation. (Matthew 12:45)

I met him in February of 2011. He stepped down from the tractor he was driving and towered at 6'2", well groomed, shirt tucked in, face clean- neatly trimmed and spoke with a massive voice. Even with the dirt on him, he was still presentable. This mature man was not my usual cup of tea, and maybe that was part of the attraction. Maturity, a hard worker, no one's slouch, he may just know how to treat a lady. Hmmm, and that he did.

Even though he watched and waited silently for a while, when he finally approached me, he was very aggressive and persistent. He inquired about purchasing a car he saw in my yard which he really had no interest in; it was a "reason" to talk to me. From that conversation, I gave him my phone number. I should have listened to my gut; my inner-self.

The perfect gentleman is how he presented himself. Opening doors, taking my hand to guide my step, offering me his jacket if it were chilly (which is rather funny if you saw the two of us together), then to end the night with a sweet kiss on the hand. Even after we parted ways he'd call me to make sure I made it home safely. He showered me with attention and compliments that I had longed for. He was kind and thoughtful; always giving gifts refusing to take no for an answer. Shortly after we met, I let him in on my personal life. I wasn't working at the time and my unemployment had been depleted; he insisted on helping me out financially. I thought it was a blessing from above, but subsequently learned that with him, all things came with a price. My mother used to say, "don't take anything from a man, and you won't have to feel like you owe him anything back". I had always used this advice, until now.

He would also routinely tell me that his deceased mother had sent me to him as an angel. He explained how it had to be destined for us to be together. The timing and location fit perfectly together like a jigsaw puzzle. Oh, I missed the part where he had chiseled the edges. He got into my head and had me believing what he wanted me to

Transition: Ashes Emanating Beauty

believe. Before I knew anything, we were cohabitating. I wasn't so sure on how we had gotten to that point, but I was even more confused about how to get out of it.

He constantly showered me with compliments in public and especially in private. He continued to open doors, he would not allow me to carry anything other than my purse and he checked the car daily to make sure it was safe and roadworthy. If it was cold, he would go out early and start the car so I would not have to sit in the cold as the car heated up. On rainy days, he would walk me to the car holding an umbrella for me, hand it to me, and walk back to the house in the rain with nothing. Please, don't let me forget to say, on payday, he gave his check to be put right back in the household budget immediately after Uncle Sam got his. He wouldn't have it any other way. I believed he genuinely cared about my safety and well-being; I still believe that to be true today.

He was definitely a working man, he was a farmer. With farm work, the weather also must do her part. So, when it rains, there is no work. In the dead of winter, again, there is no work. On the days, he did not work, he cooked a full meal and washed all the clothes and cleaned the house. If there was ever anything that needed to be done, he did it. He felt that by 7:00 o'clock in the morning everybody in the world should be awake, dressed and ready to get the day started; and that's letting you sleep late. What a wonderful world.

I saw red flags from time to time, and reasoned them away. After all, there is a reasonable explanation for everything if you just take time to think about it, right? A man that does all the things I described would not and could not have another side. Especially not one with an anger problem triggered by drinking or sometimes a lack thereof. No, not this mature man, he can't be verbally abusive and outright disrespectful. The one who showers me with compliments. The one who allows me to stay in a woman's place and not have to do anything he considers to be a man's job (in the physical sense; nothing sexist).

I believe the man is the head of the house and I would never want to do or say anything to step out of my place but this very thing, even with the best of intentions, was used against me. From anger to insults; insults to disrespect; disrespect to intimidation if I talked of leaving. This was my private life. He knew one thing, I never wanted to make a scene. Often, he used it against me. Even more so than that, he wanted the outside world to view him as that perfect guy.

Transition: Ashes Emanating Beauty

How did I ever get here? Oh, I remember, I let him in. Never in a million years would I think I would ever be a single mother, not once, but twice. I had dreams of my mother making wedding plans and my father giving me away. No, never in a million years did I think I'd be in this situation. Wow, what a bed I've made. I lie down on shards of glass and nails with a cylinder block for a pillow. When in public, I would just grin and take it even though my soul was being shredded. You say you love me, and you wish you could give me the world, yet you refuse to speak to me with sweet lips even if we disagree. The shift happened right in front of my eyes.

I am a firm believer that we should be able to talk it out without falling out. In the right setting, if you push me, I will push back and that is not the woman I want to be. I feel I should not have to be put in the position to be on the defensive in my home. I should not have to go to the extreme to readjust my character to fit his ever-changing mood if things/life was not going the way he wanted but I did. I acted in that manner to keep down any type of confusion whatsoever. I even went so far as to interact differently with my children on the same accord. There was a level of jealousy that he would never admit to. He was jealous of anything that took away from his time with me, be it my children, church, my parents or my sisters.

The only thing he was willing to tolerate taking away from "our time" was me going to work. Everything I wanted to do was second-guessed. I was not able to make any decisions, not because I was told not to; I had become insecure within myself. I was alone; I was too embarrassed for anyone to know what I was dealing with. Most of the time, our communication was handicapped. How I felt was never validated. Nothing I did was ever good enough. Regardless, if it is right or wrong, how you feel is how you feel. If I talked to him about how I felt, should I be blessed with his attention, someone else smarter had to tell me how I was supposed to feel. I had an overwhelming sense of un-appreciation. I began to make a mess of things that I could naturally do well prior to our relationship. I was a complete mess and things were getting worse.

I never had black eyes, nor did I mask bruises. He never punched me with his fist, but he did slap me; I slapped him back. He found out that day I used to be a tomboy. Though I was that tom boy, I am still a lady. Some battles, I should not have to fight. His constant and consistent complaining about every little thing made me very insecure. I was always on pins and needles. Did I do it

Transition: Ashes Emanating Beauty

right? Will he like this? One of my greatest fears had always been of being a statistic. I never wanted to be anybody's pushover. Even with that deep inside me, I was always concerned about the "what if" factor. What if one day he did some of the many ugly things he said he would do? His words, they cut so deep and precise, finishing with "And I know what I am saying". As if to say, don't blame it on the alcohol later. Like clockwork, he'd come back and say he was sorry and he could never mean those things. I wondered to myself, how many times could you stand to hear that "Apolo*lie" (a false apology) before it became a deafening joke.

In a lot of ways, he was a good man. He's a good man with a substance abuse problem and even worse, he had a bad disposition about life, which I'm not sure are linked together. One bad addiction feeding off the other. The things he would say would take me straight to church. I could see the evil in his eyes and hear Lucifer in his voice. Those aforementioned scriptures were more real than ever now. You know, **wrestling not against flesh and blood** and all. But then I'd hear "***Jesus I know, and Paul I know; but who are ye?***" I knew I didn't want the evil spirit in him to jump on me and send me running naked from the house all because I am trying to command respect from a demon and he knows I am not where I should be with the Lord. The enemy will set you up or even let you set yourself up and laugh at you in the end.

    We had an on and off again relationship for about six years. With each break, I'd say I'm never going back. I can finally breathe. I'm free. I'm done. He would say whatever was necessary to get me to talk. He knew if I talked to him, he'd say something to make me smile, then eventually to laugh. Next, he would make sure he gave me the money that he knew I needed. He would begin to date me all over again. I would remember all the good times, and reconcile the bad. It was always good before it got bad. Each time we made up, the intensity of our bond grew stronger. We were more alike in many ways and different in others. But when things would start to take a turn for the worse, he would just go all in instead of folding and somehow, so did I. If life and death is in the tongue, crime scene tape would stretch around the perimeter.

    He grew up in a time where he had to learn to be a man at an early age. The eldest of eight brothers and sisters and a helper to mom. I imagine that it all plays a role in the man that he is today. But that's no excuse, not any more.

Transition: Ashes Emanating Beauty

People have often said when evaluating your relationship, make a list of the good and of the bad. If the good outweighs the bad, then it's a good relationship. If the bad outweighs the good, maybe not so much. For my situation, neither of these were helping the case. Maybe my scale needed readjusting or it is out right broken. Certainly, by numbers, the good outweighs the bad; but who's to say how you do your math?

It's been seven months, and he still calls me several times a day to ask me how I am and to let me know he loves me. The first few months were tough. Filled with veiled threats. Then the next few weeks, he was dying from cancer. Next, he'd get miraculously healed in a few days. Then he just wants someone to talk to because he's so lonely. He has offered plenty of gifts and in my desperate time of need, I refused. I have at least learned "all money ain't good money". Some people may not see this as a struggle but it is. I was not raised in a home where I had to deal with these challenges, and I am forever grateful.

I have been getting to know the person who has been watching me for 44 years waiting to be discovered. She silently tells me that I am worth so much more than the things that I have been offered and given permission to in life. I deserve more than to be called out of my name

Permission Granted

during times of frustration. I deserve to be loved and listened to; hugged and hoped for. If nothing else, I have learned that *"For greater is He that is in me, than he that is in the world."*

To my boys, for every argument, distasteful and disrespectful word that you had to hear, I offer my deepest apologies. I love you.

"I am learning to love the sound of my feet walking away from things not for me!" - Unknown

Tyree L Groves

Living a Shade of Gray

"Love recognizes no barriers. It jumps hurdles, leaps fences, penetrates walls to arrive at its destination full of hope."-Maya Angelou

Has life ever thrown you a curve ball that changed everything? What would you do if everything changed your love life, but it made you feel better? Would you deny your private life to save you from public opinion?

"He just wants you to be his maid." I looked over at my aunt. I could not believe she said that. "What the hell? Is this the 1950's?" Getting up from her couch in disgust, I left out the door.

Dating outside of my race seemed almost normal to me. I had grown up in California for the most part with all cultures and races so I didn't understand the animosity. In fact, my first "boyfriend" was Filipino. But here I was in Louisiana where things were and continue to be separate. Black men dated white women and no one really batted an eye, except in my family. There were no interracial relationships, and no mixed children.

My family still had an old-world view of things. Some of them still used terms like *white folks* and *them people*. Even though outwardly no one was "racist" there was still a separatist mentality. It wasn't anything we sat around discussing at the dinner table, but it was understood. Black people stayed with black people.

It was hard enough for me to admit to my "black love" family that I had been dating a guy who wasn't black. In fact, I had been in a relationship with a white man for about six months at that point and I wanted to bring him around. I knew there would be some issues, I didn't expect it to be so blatant. So, I finally dropped the bomb. Maybe the word bomb was too soft. It was more like a nuclear reaction. I had violated the most sacred "unsaid" rule and crossed that invisible line.

What was the problem? I was grown, why did I have to hide this relationship? Because they weren't ready? Because it went against that "strong black women support strong black men" stigma that I learned since being in Louisiana? If my aunt who loved me and supported me in everything reacted like this, how was the rest of the family going to react? I was not looking forward to it. I didn't deal with most of my family for one reason or another, so their opinions didn't matter to me.

But suddenly, everyone had an opinion on my relationship status. I became the conversation at the dinner table because I was dating a *white boy*. Before, when I was married to a man who I had to fight every three weeks like clockwork, nobody had anything to say. If they did, no one cared enough to say anything to me about it.

What they didn't care to understand was I had never been in an abusive relationship before and was so traumatized I had PTSD. *PTSD (post-traumatic stress disorder), a mental health problem that some people develop after experiencing or witnessing a life-threatening event, like combat, a natural disaster, a car accident, or sexual assault (*www.ptsd.va.gov*)*. The trauma of that relationship created a deep fear of black men. When I say deep, I mean deep. It was embarrassing to say that, but it was true at that time.

If I saw a man that resembled my ex-husband, I had a panic attack. They could have been dark skinned like him or tall like him or skinny like him. It didn't matter, in my mind all of *them* were alike and my body reacted violently to the point of having nightmares. That didn't seem like a normal reaction and I knew I had to get over it, but in the meantime, I could not date another black man.

That fear gripped me and affected my entire being. How can I fear men who looked like me? How can I raise my son to be proud of who he is and I feared that very thing he was growing up to be? Fear no one but God, I said over and over to myself. Praying to get that negative memory out of my head and heart for the sake of my son was a daily routine.

As I predicted, my family was not supportive. "How are you going to raise a black man with a white man?" One of my family members asked in a joking, but not really joking way. My response, "My son can never question that he is a black male, he knows that. As long as he is raised to be a man, that is all I care about." Plenty of single black mothers have accomplished this with no man in sight. It became apparent, my family was not ready for this "big" change. My favorite uncle even became short with me. Even though he never verbalized his disapproval, I saw it in his face. Dealing with my family was one thing, my ex-husband was another. He started stalking me and I had to move out of the parish to get away from him. I was dealing with enough in my life with the family and the ex. Thinking I was finally going to be happy since I was away from both, was naïve.

I never cared what people thought about me because generally it wasn't told to me. However, when you are in an interracial relationship people take off the filters. They don't care what they say and most think they have the right to let you know how they feel about it. Maybe it was a southern thing, people stayed with "their own." I can understand that, especially because you can drive into certain areas of Louisiana and are reminded of slavery. Plantations that used to harbor slaves and have horrible things happen, now serve as tourist attractions. We have all heard the stories of the *"house nigga"*, the pretty one that massa picked to be "his." That is what people thought? This wasn't about love, but about redoing history to feel picked? Maybe for some black women it was true, for me it was about feeling safe and loved.

Work was no different, my coworkers asked inappropriate questions. "What is the sex like?" "Are they different from black men?" "Does he spoil you?" "How does his family treat you?" Would they ask that if I was dating a black guy? Probably not. People felt they had a right to invade my privacy and I was their own personal google. I have heard stereotypes like white guys had smaller penises, they just like the exoticness of black women, or white men are extra crazy. Some stereotypes have a root to them; that much I understand. I believe a man is a man and the size of a man's penis is more scientific than race, but then again, I can't speak for every male because I haven't seen every male's penis. As a black woman, I never considered myself "exotic" because of my

Transition: Ashes Emanating Beauty

race. Are white men crazier than black men? Crazy is crazy, that much isn't race based. The real differences between them is not as obvious.

    Black men and older white people looked at us like we committed a crime. Sometimes, I would get frustrated and depending on how I was feeling that day would determine the reaction they would get. Sometimes I would just ignore them unless the ignorance was blatant. Men that would normally look, smile and keep it moving would see me with this white man and all respect went out of the window. They would make it obvious they were looking, sometimes making comments or touching me. Many times, I had to calm a situation down and we had to leave a place because things got heated. After a while of dating him, either people stopped staring or I stopped noticing. Either way, the relationship got serious. When my family recognized that I was happy and my son was too, they relaxed. Since his family had a lot of interracial dating and children, the relationship wasn't an issue for them. At least the issues weren't about me being black but there were other issues.

    The funny thing is during that time, my fear of black men went away but something else changed. Now, like any other woman, I appreciate good looks but it wasn't the same as before. I was no longer attracted to black men in the same way. It was like admiring a dress on someone else but knowing you would not want to wear it. Maybe it was the type of black men I was running into. It seemed like they were aggressive, or ex-cons, or married and wanted a "friend." Not like that mattered, I was in a relationship. Things were good for a while, but like I said, there were other issues in the relationship. He started to become over possessive which I was not going through again. These issues lead to me cheating and eventually leaving him. I had to find me, I had bounced from an abusive relationship to a possessive one. It didn't make sense how I made a 180 degree turn in my dating life and still ended up with men who had similar qualities.

While finding me, I was still dating but just one side of the spectrum. One day I had an honest discussion with a male coworker. He had noticed how I dealt with black men versus white men. We were friends so I didn't get offended. He said I treated white men like I was open to dating and black men more like brothers. Was this true? Not to me, but to him it was. He said I was intimidating to all men, but with black men I seemed guarded. I wasn't trying to be, it just seemed like none of the ones I met, fit me. I only dated what I thought fit me.

Transition: Ashes Emanating Beauty

Dating interracially causes you to deal with many things most people don't understand. Surprisingly, I dated one guy who was looking for the "exotic" black woman experience. His family had their own feelings about black people. He had never dated a black woman before. I heard stereotypes that they repeated to him and he repeated to me. Black women were all about money. Black women beat their men. The stereotypes and disrespect also came from his exes and his kid's mothers. Tell your "nigger bitch" this that or the other. Of course, these things were not said to my face but the fact that he didn't defend me ended that relationship. It also made me add some requirements to my interracial dating. If they had never brought a black woman home, I was not going to be the first! That was years ago, I don't know if my sisterly behavior towards black men changed, but I hadn't dated one since my abusive ex-husband. The ones who approached me in my single life, that would be up to the standards I set, seemed to always be attached.

My son had gotten older and men seemed crazier than usual. My plan was to enjoy the single dating life, nothing serious, just fun. Life had other plans and I met the man who changed my life. It all started with a dating app. I was just looking for someone to pass time, so the color didn't matter. But it was like grocery shopping. I had my preferences set and that included race. "Those who wander are not always lost" is what the caption on his dating profile said. Interesting quote, I never heard it before, but I knew it had to be a quote. I looked at his pictures, he had kids and one was obviously mixed. Whew! No need to ask that "do you date" or "have you ever dated" question. Due to the past, that would have had to be addressed, I was not going through the redneck mentality again. He was attractive and looked like he would be fun. Someone who could take my mind off the residue of previous relationships.

  I was ready to delete the app and just not date. Some of the things men said and did through those apps were ridiculous. To be honest, I received enough "inappropriate" pictures to fill a magazine. But there was something about him so I bit the bullet and responded, "some of them are lost" and it was a done deal. I wasn't sure if he would respond back. My response was weird, plus I didn't even have a picture up just words on my profile. Even though I was not looking for anything serious, I wanted someone who wanted to get to know me not just respond because of what I looked like.

Transition: Ashes Emanating Beauty

He responded! The first night, we talked all night as he was working and stayed up when he got off to talk more. We talked for a while before I sent him a picture of me. He was different. He didn't seem hard up like some of the other guys I had talked to. He was open, but he had been hurt and wasn't looking to get serious either. We were on one accord with that. Fun, exclusive but not seriously committed.

When we finally decided to meet in person, I discovered he lived five minutes from me. We got to know each other and months later decided we were going to be committed. When his job sent him out of state to work, it became unbearable for us not to see each other. Was this love? If it was, I apparently never felt it before. Craig was more different than anyone I ever had met. Since we were only a few hours away, I figured I could go and start visiting him on the weekends, so that meant I had to tell my son. Kamrin was in 10th grade at the time. He was close to my ex and I didn't want to bring anyone else into his life he wasn't ready for. I gave him the option of deciding when he wanted to meet him. When they met, I was moving to a bigger apartment and Craig came by to help before he had to go to work. That is the type of man he is, willing to lose sleep to make my life easier. Craig was cool and so was

Kamrin. There was no weirdness, just my son sizing him up like a son would do.

Their relationship grew organically, just like ours did. Before I "fully" committed, I had to see how his family would act; most of all how his kids were. Like I said earlier, I started to set some requirements. If I didn't like the kids, it didn't matter how much I loved him, all serious relationship thoughts were going out the window. Surprisingly, his family embraced us from the beginning. They loved us and treated us better than my own family. They said, Craig had a few destructive behaviors before we started dating, he had changed and they appreciated me for that. He knew from us talking before we started dating, I was not going for any craziness. Life has a funny way of directing you the way you are supposed to go. Our relationship grew and we got engaged. Something both of us said we would never do again! I couldn't deny that I had found my soulmate. The one God created for me.

My life had to go the way it did, otherwise I don't know if I would have been truly open to dating him. People still stare; that hasn't changed, I just don't notice as much. We often get asked "are you guys together" at the checkout line and sometimes will get asked inappropriate questions. Regrettably, there have been people who have had to be put out of our lives, both family and friends. We are like any "normal" couple, but society hasn't changed much. In fact, with all the racial issues that have happened over the last few years, we have been put in some awkward positions. There have even been racist inboxes informing me that I should be ashamed of myself for being with a white man. Do I get pissed? Yes, of course and I react in a nice/nasty way. At the end of the day, this is my family. We love and respect each other and will have each other's back regardless of the opposition. That is what makes us solid. Race has nothing to do with that. Regardless of the race of the person we choose to date or marry, love is love and don't let anyone tell you different or make you feel bad about it.

"Have enough courage to trust love one more time and always one more time"-Maya Angelou

Valencia Griffin-Wallace

Trapped in the Jewelry Box

As far back as I can remember I lived my life to please others. Like living the life of a toy ballerina inside a jewelry box, spinning around for everyone to see. I was controlled by the thoughts, comments and opinions of others. Just like the ballerina, I served no purpose until someone opened the lid of the box and whined me up to see me spin around to the music. Once the fun stopped they simply closed the lid and went on their way leaving me lonely inside a dark box.

Living in the entrapped cycle of my life caused me to grow up being a people pleaser. Having no real sense of reality and not understanding that everyone I tried to please really did not cared about pleasing me. As a confused child, with no sense of direction, I acted on the opinions of others. I allowed myself to be placed in many difficult situations that took me years to overcome. Being a people pleaser, I felt like I had to please someone all the time. I remember one day my parents took me over my grandmother's house dressed in all white. I was always dressed like that but I didn't see the problem until I was told I could not play with my friends. My instructions were, "do not move from off granny's porch you're too clean to go and play with those *little ugly dirty kids.*" From that point on those words became my reality. The other children were *little ugly dirty kids* and I was the *little pretty girl*. Even though, in the back of my mind, I wanted to play and get dirty with the other kids; I wanted to be normal. I knew asking my parents to change my clothes so I could play would only upset them. My mom's motto was to always look pretty and smile regardless of how you felt on the inside. I was taught to care about my outward appearance.

Living life in a false reality I was forced to suppress my true feelings if they do not line up with how others felt. I had become the ballerina in the jewelry box and didn't even know it; spinning around looking pretty for everyone to see. Just think about it for a second, the ballerina is placed inside a dark box controlled by someone opening and closing the lid. God showed me that my life was the same as the ballerina inside the box but, I had to get tired and stop spinning to regain control of my life.

I had allowed people to deposit lies inside my head by telling me because I was pretty I didn't need to think for myself; look pretty and you will get someone to do everything for you. So, I believed that. I must admit it worked for a while but, just like the ballerina in the box, I did not know - no matter how pretty you are on the outside you still can be hollow and empty on the inside. I did not know when a person is done watching you spin they will cut you off or simply close the lid. The music inside the jewelry box continued to play but no one can see the pretty little ballerina anymore. Eventually, the music fades away. And that's exactly what happened to me. At nine years old I was adopted and my last name changed. I had no knowledge of the adoption until one day I was told to start writing my new name at school. I was so confused and emotionally unsure what was wrong with my original last name. I was too young to really understand. My thoughts were, "Who am I? What does this adoption have to do with me?" This was only the start of my "issues of life."

Have you ever thought that maybe the individual you're allowing to control your actions want to be you? When they look in the mirror they want to see you instead of themselves. They sit back and watch how you respond to other people's actions so they know exactly what to do based on your response. Some things never change!

My family's motto was smile, wear elegant clothing, do not embarrass me, get good grades so that you can make lots of money and get a husband to take care of you. What they were really telling me was to smile so that people won't see my pain, wear elegant clothing so you can look like you're something that you're not, don't embarrass me, get good grades so I can brag to my friends about it, make lots of money because once you go down the road of destruction you're going to need it and get a husband so I can control your family through him. Living up to my family's motto led me into "the devil's playground."

    I learned my outer appearance was an easy way to gain attention from men. I began living a very promiscuous life; having sex at an early age. In doing so, I received some very harsh beatings that left me with black eyes, body bruises, neck braces and lies to cover up the abuse from the local authorities. Those experiences took me on a roller coaster ride. I was always moving from house to house with different family members. After, experiencing years of abuse I had gained a false sense of what love meant. I believed if I did things to make people react that meant they loved me. By the time I was 14 years old I wanted to have a baby. I thought the baby would make someone love me. I started running the streets and selling drugs just to fit in. Hurt by the several sexual encounters that left me empty, I often wondered; "Will I ever find someone to love me unconditionally?" Perplexed by a false sense of what true love meant and wondering why I haven't found someone to love me yet I thought that if I could only get married, start my own family and make some money I would be happy; that was my perception.

Trapped in the Jewelry Box

At 17, after having a one nightstand, I ended up getting pregnant with my first child and contemplated abortion. I thought having a baby would make a man happy, and he seemed like he really cared for me. He was telling me he would die for me and he would give me his last breath. Oh, boy wasn't I naive? In the most uncertain fearful time of my life, I decided to keep the baby. Here I am a teen parent, living with my daughter's father on welfare; determined to prove I could make the best of my situation. I started college but, because I had no real income I dropped out to get a job to support my daughter. I never realized when someone wanted to control your life they'll use anything they can against you. I remember I had saved up enough money to purchase my daughter's first Easter dress on my own. It wasn't a lot of money but, it was the best I could do. My mother did not like the Easter dress she told me to take it back and she would buy the dress she liked. When I said no, she threatened to take the car she had given me. When I think back on that situation I would've never thought, in a million years, I could lose my car because I bought my daughter an inexpensive Easter dress. Emotionally hurt and feeling trapped by choosing between a car or my personal freedom drove my people pleasing habits into overload. My thought was "I need to make more money to purchase elegant clothes." From that day forward I continued doing everything based on what other people thought by any means necessary.

First Marriage

    I thought having another baby would make my daughter's father happy and we would get married and raise our children together. Finally, I would be happy, right? I convinced him to marry me by complaining to him that we were living in sin and I wanted my two daughters to have the same father. I did not want to be alone and I wanted everyone to think I finally made it from being a teen parent to a wife. I married my first husband thinking I'm going to do better than anyone else in my family. All of my children will have the same father, my family will be so proud of me, and my husband will love me forever. Well, the day after the wedding my new husband and I got into a physical altercation over another woman and both of us were kicked out of the hotel that we were staying at for our honeymoon. After the fight, he left me on the Las Vegas strip to fend for myself and I did not see him until we boarded the plane the next day. I had no money so once again I had to depend on someone else for help. My sister's mother, who was there for the wedding gave me $20.00 to catch a cab to the Las

Trapped in the Jewelry Box

Vegas airport. After sitting in the airport for 12 hours waiting on my return flight home I was still determined to make my marriage work. I was thinking "Do I allow my decisions to be controlled by what other people will think or do I move on and learn from my mistakes?" At that moment, my actions were controlled by what I thought others would think of me.

    I stayed in the relationship for a total of 12 years enduring physical, verbal, mental, and emotional abuse; topped with adultery because I didn't want to be looked at as a failure. Not to mention, all these forms of abuse were the norm in my upbringing; you do something wrong you get hit, you fight then make up, even if it results in criminal matters, or permanent scars. This was just the way real love is right?" Wrong! During all this time I also, allowed his mother to control and manipulate me by giving me things such as stoves, beds, cooking utensils, and even a brand-new car. Do you see the pattern? The things she helped me with always had a hidden clause in it. I say that because as long as I was with her son she was on my side but the second I wanted to leave she tried to take back everything she gave me and took his side. Once again, I chose the help over freedom because I was determined to show my family I did not need anything from them. I continued to accept help from his mother and became enslaved to him and her and I paid for it years later.

Insecurities

Most people viewed me as a pretty, talented, well-put-together woman not knowing deep down inside I suffered with a lot of insecurities. There's an old saying, *everything that glitters ain't gold* and boy did I make myself glitter for people." I put on a façade like I had it all together hiding behind a fake smile, sexy clothing, expensive shoes and purses. I pretended nothing bad was going on in my life. There were times a simple decision such as what to wear caused me so much stress because I worried about how people would view my outward appearance. Whether good or bad I tended to care what other people thought of me. I told myself, "If they were mad it was because they were jealous but if people were good I patted myself on the back as if to say, "job well done." Either way I made it so at the end of the day I won. I never realized the people pleasing mentality I lived in was bad until I saw my children starting down the same road of destruction. My children were becoming trapped inside the jewelry box by the same people that had me trapped. My husband and my children were all controlled by others at some point in life trying to gain the necessary attention from others. "Who am I?" This lonely little girl inside a jewelry box we call life living in a perpetual state of overload, depression, discouragement, stretched to the limit and on the verge of collapse.

It's My Decision

I always wanted to become an entrepreneur but that did not fit into the family "Motto." In 2006, I decided to quit my job at the hospital to start working at my home running a daycare full time. Not knowing all the business aspects of entrepreneurship, I faked it until I made it but it was not easy. I knew how to smile and I had mastered my people pleasing skills so I made people feel very comfortable with me. It was a recipe for my success. The business was doing excellent, I was even able to expand to a commercial location. I felt like I was on the top of the world. I had become a successful business owner, a wife with three beautiful children that was making my own money, plus a faithful Christian. I should be happy, right? But, I wasn't something was still missing – *"What about me; what was I doing; who are you?"* I asked myself. My life was still being controlled by the cares of other people, facing abuse because I had not changed my thought process. My life was still the same, looking good on the outside empty on the inside.

What's next?

I thought that if I add more success, money, and status to my life it would fill the void inside of me and the pain would go away. I wanted us to become foster parents to appear that we had it all together. Even though I did it for all the right reasons and it looked good on the outside, it still left me empty on the inside. I was still trapped in a marriage that was never built on a solid foundation and I wanted out. Scared of what God and people would think of me if I left I stayed while secretly trying to find some happiness for myself. I started drinking heavily, partying and going to the club that soon led me to commit adultery. Even though I knew my husband had been cheating on me I never planned on doing the same. I was lost. I was trying anything to cover up my pain. I soon realized that all the alcohol, drugs and sex in the world could not help how I truly felt on the inside. Not even the attention from men. As long as people were feeding into my insecurities I believed I was fine. Regrettably, this only led me to place myself inside a bigger box where I was trapped by my own perceptions relying on other people's opinions to validate who I was.

60 Minutes

Then it happened. One day, in 2007, I reached my breaking point. I told myself, no longer was I going to live my life controlled by other people's thoughts and opinions and I was ready to leave. I was terrified because of a recent altercation between my husband and I. All my clothing was destroyed but, I did not let that stop me. I called my uncle and told him, I had one hour to move my remaining things before he made it home. I had secretly gotten a new apartment. I left that day, with only the clothes on my back, my three children, one couch, one bed, and an old washer and dryer. I was tired of putting on a fake façade trying to get a positive reaction from people including my husband; all to fuel my insecurities. At this point, I did not care what people thought about me because I had God. I said, "God I don't know what I'm doing, but because you said it was time for me to leave, I'm going to ride it till the wheels fall off. I was out in 60 minutes or less. I filed for divorce and began living life without any cares in the world. Amid getting a divorce, I fell deeply in love with the man who I am married to today. However, before we were married I found myself still looking for people to notice me. Again, I found myself trying to live for people rather than focusing on my true happiness.

After the 1st divorce

Living with the love of my life shacking up with our five children. Sounds like the good life, right? Sometimes at night I would wake up screaming at the top of my lungs seeing the vision of myself trapped inside a jewelry box with no way out. Inside the box were all my purses, clothes, jewelry, shoes, and I was naked. Had I wandered off to a place of no return? I was thinking "how do I get back to a familiar place?" But I remember telling God, "I'm going to ride it to the wheels fall off." Had I become the puppet controlling the puppeteer creating my own show?

My life was focused on spending enormous amounts of money on clothes, getting my hair done, alcohol, car rentals, clubbing, wild partying and smoking. I was on top of the world again, right? All of these external things still did not bring about acceptance. In fact, because I was not under my ex-husband and his mother's control anymore they joined forces to come against me. They took me to court alleging that I was causing my children emotional distress. They had my kids go along with it to gain control of me again. Those allegations forced the licensing bureau to close my daycare business and child protective services had compiled a case to remove my children from my care. Because of this I contemplated going back to my ex-husband. Yes, back to where I had been physically, emotionally, verbally and mentally abused; if that would make everyone else happy including my kids, then so be it!

I couldn't seem to find my way after the divorce. BUT GOD! I owe it all to My God! After, praying God showed me that He has the last say in everything! The allegations were dropped and I could resume my daycare business. Still angry at the individuals who caused me to almost lose everything, I was determined to show everyone that I was good. I closed the business and returned to work traditional with no real intentions of staying. I only wanted to prove I wasn't a failure. Within, one year I became the Manager of the company and started working from home. My perception was success in any type of way would make me feel better and people wouldn't see me as a failure.

The darkest hour

Worrying about how other people felt about me shacking up, in addition to how God felt I had to ask myself the question, "Am I ever going to get married again?" This lifestyle was all wrong for me. I was living with someone without real commitment. I believe that is one of the worst things you can do in a relationship. On the other hand, lying to yourself, painting the picture to outsiders like you're in a committed relationship when you are not, can be just as devastating. One day the reality of living without commitment to each other showed its ugly face. I found out the man I was living with was seeing someone else. I had known deep down inside but I just didn't want to believe it. I was crushed! I knew I couldn't hold it against him because I was doing the same. I had been allowing myself to live in a world that I knew nothing about. Loving someone, so much that you accept things in life you really don't want is not good.

    I knew he loved me but was just as afraid as I was of getting his heart broken again. He too, had just gone through a failed marriage. I think I was more embarrassed than hurt. When it happened my first thought was, *"What are people going to think and say about me now?"* My mind told me I must go out and show people that I'm okay and act like the situation do not happen. That did not work because people let me know that they knew it did. Then God showed up again for me. He took away the pain for the both of us, "yes us". He was just as hurt as I was. I realize I could not play the victim alone. This time was different I could not keep lying to myself, I had to face the truth and I had to lay my true feelings out on the table and tell him what I really wanted was to be his wife and nothing less.

My Second Marriage

Finally, we got married and had a beautiful wedding but the baggage of my past was still haunting me. So, fascinated with title of being a wife again I began to look at life like it was a game and I was winning. I knew deep down inside my *"people pleasing"* had to be dealt with to truly be happy and remain married to the love of my life. However, I did not know where to start. I was still living on the fence not totally free from that mind set. When I was promoted at my current employer my head was so big. I did not see that it would trap me inside the box again. I would often find myself still doing things like boasting about my new house, my car and husband, following up with "oh, we go to church every Sunday too" not realizing what I had just done. Often my husband would encourage me to live life for me and not for people. Showing me that if we were going to build a long-lasting life together, I had to break free and stop worrying about others and quit playing their game altogether.

My change process

After listening to one of my employees say, *"I watch people, wait to see how you respond to things just to see the reaction on your face."* I had heard this several times from my husband so I asked her to further explain what she meant. She gave me her published workbooks *The Process of Change; A Look at Me, Love Yourself and Moving Forward.* While on a mission's cruise in the middle of the Caribbean Ocean I read her book and one question in her workbook titled *Love yourself* stated, "Tell the truth about your life." It was like a judge was standing before me mandating me to release my past and I had no other choice but to deal with it. I began writing in small segments asking myself questions like," Where did all this start?" The question from the book helped me to tell the truth about how I really felt about different situations, my children, my family, my marriage, my job, my adulterous relationships, my spirituality and myself. Then I had to deal with the pedestal I had place myself on, acting as if my life hasn't had any bumps, bruises, hurt, bad decisions and shame. I had to accept my entire life not just parts of it and ask God forgiveness.

I had to admit that for years I had no intention to change. I allowed my behavior to be controlled by other people opinions, comments, past hurt and actions. My behavior was unmotivated and I avoided any information, discussion, regarding changing. I had to admit up to this point of my life I was really living to please others; trying to paint a perfect picture rather than allowing God to use His perfect plan to shape me. In my opinion, people pleasing is like an addiction. When overcoming it you must take it one day at a time. **Be aware of your motivates** and quickly make the necessary adjustments not to fall back into a trap. Through my relationship with God I had to learn to accept the good, the bad and the ugly moments of the past. Although some of it was out of my control, to make sure I did not take on a victim mentality I had to remember I allowed my actions to be controlled by others. I had to accept the things I could not change and move on. Sitting and writing this story reminds me how great God is and his grace is sufficient for any situation.

I have finally relieved myself from other people's expectations by digging deep within myself. After, praying, fasting, understanding my why in life, and learning Jesus died just for me so I could be free, I was able to move forward. I gained a lot of self-clarity and discovered the true issue that allowed me to be controlled. Once I heard a pastor say, *"Find the chief or it will return."* My chief (the root cause) was my own lack of self-worth, lack of identity, fear, doubt, anger, rage, perfectionism, unforgiveness embedded by other people plans they had for my life.

Ask yourself this question: How do you see yourself in your world? Truth is, the only perception you have control over is your own. I had to eliminate my false reality of other people's perceptions and find God's expectation according to; Jeremiah 1:5-10 (Message Bible):

***5** Before I shaped you in the womb, I knew all about you. Before you saw the light of day, I had holy plans for you: A prophet to the nations— that's what I had in mind for you." **6** But I said, "Hold it, Master God! Look at me. I don't know anything. I'm only a boy!" **7-8** God told me, "Don't say, 'I'm only a boy.' I'll tell you where to go and you'll go there. I'll tell you what to say and you'll say it. Don't be afraid of a soul. I'll be right there, looking after you." God's Decree. **9-10** God reached out, touched my mouth, and said, "Look! I've just put my words in our mouth—hand-delivered! See what I've done? I've given you a job to do among nations and governments—a red-*

letter day! Your job is to pull up and teardown, take apart and demolish, and then start over, building and planting."

After, I understood GOD's expectation for my life things began to change. The layers of bondage were relieved which initiated a spiritual awakening. This new spiritual awakening has allowed me to see reality rather than false perceptions. I have minor relapse days but I'm alert and the layers of bondage continue to be removed daily. Finally, positive everlasting change, freedom, and true happiness are in motion. I encourage you to find your current emotional state and personal triggers to maintain your freedom and avoid relapsing.

Through my journey and mindset shift I have created my own Life Motto: Determination, Endurance, Perseverance & Truth equals Happiness (DEPTH) and now I have the FREEDOM TO MOVE FORWARD WITH IDENTITY AND PURPOSE!

I believe these seven tips can help you began to reshape your mindset and your life:

1. Be honest with yourself through your process; know and accept the truth always. Change is a process that is implemented in steps; **Identify your current stage of change and work towards freedom;**

Transition: Ashes Emanating Beauty

Precontemplation, Contemplation, Preparation, Action, Maintenance, and Termination.
2. Pray sincerely. Find songs and scriptures to motivate you and listen or read them daily. Remove all masks before asking for help.
3. Work with your shortcomings never view them as negative; remember they're a part of you. Your trials and tribulations will help someone else.
4. Accept the things you cannot change; family included. Remove yourself from negative people or situations that may cause you to relapse.
5. Learn from your mistakes and failures.
6. Never stop dreaming; dream with purpose. Write out your vision with clear goals and create an action plan to achieve them.
7. Be happy where you are and never compare your process to someone else's because you don't know their story.

Tasheikya Hunter

The Survival Game

As a Gemini, many say I have Twins within, one reserved and intelligent and the other clever and mean. Who would have known that a small-town country girl would have nine lives with seven already spent? Flint, Michigan native, raised in the small community called Beecher by my mom as a single parent. My parents divorced when I was three years old. I had five older siblings. I was about 12 years old when my older sister left the house and went to college. From that point on I was basically raised as a single child. I didn't have the type of siblings that would come back and check on my well-being or do anything with me so I made my own way.

In school, I was the type of kid that was a loner. I socialized sometimes. Around the age of 15, I became a product of my environment and begun to sell crack. I hung around with older young men, traveled back and forth to Detroit, and sold to some of my classmate's parents. I was always around grown people and was fearless. I was a gifted and talented A & B student. In the 8th grade, I scored high on the SAT which was rewarded with the opportunity to attend Michigan Tech in a summer program and complete a computer programming course. I had the potential to soar academically instead of selling drugs if I had had any guidance. This was a dark chapter in my life and as it turns out it was the "wick" of me understanding my purpose and the cornerstone of creating my non-profit.

My illegal behavior resulted in me missing the first week of school in every month during my senior year. My absences caused me to be one credit short in English for graduation. I walked across the stage but there was no diploma in my case. Consequently, I had to make up the credit by attending an adult education school and I ended up passing the English course with an A. The day after I completed the course and got my diploma I was still trying to sell drugs and had gotten so drunk I didn't realize my mother had packed all my belongings, put them on the back of a pickup truck with a cab, and drove me 1200 miles down south to my sister's house located in Georgia.

The Transition

I landed in Georgia drunk with six crack rocks in my pocket. When I realized where I was and I stepped out of the truck- I felt like I had landed on Plymouth Rock. The area was country, there were no sidewalks, traffic, or a lot of businesses close by. It looked country; it smelled country. I looked around and said, "well okay I'm here, whatever." Almost immediately, my sister took me to register for food stamps and to fill out an application to work with her at Taco Bell. I got the job but it felt kind of out of place; like a fish out of water. Everything was so unfamiliar. All the while, in my head, my thought was *"what am I to do with these six rocks in my pocket?"* Then one day my sister introduced me to our cousin, Harry. He was not that much older than me so after we talked awhile, I felt comfortable enough to share how I made money before moving to Georgia. He seemed cool so I handed him the dope and said, *"do something with it"*. Thinking, I can't throw away money and under the assumption he was just as thuggish as I was. All I knew was I could not take the chance of selling myself and getting caught by the police. Life as I knew it was over and there was an immediate change. So, it was time to tighten up my bootstraps and become a productive, responsible citizen.

Benchmark

I came from a small town, so even though this city was small, I experienced a culture shock. I didn't have any friends, couldn't go back to Michigan, didn't have a car, didn't know where the grocery store was located, didn't know anything. I was looking for some type of familiarity. I talked with a few friends' back home to let them know where I was and what had happened to me since I disappeared off the scene so abruptly. I resulted to speaking with an ex-boyfriend who told me that he had an aunt that lived in Atlanta and I should get in touch with her so I did. I called her and she said she would like to meet up with me and maybe I could spend the night. What I considered to be liberating ended up being Pandora's box.

Departure

One weekend in August 1991, I asked my sister if I could I go and spend the weekend with the ex's aunt. She said, "*I don't care; it's fine if you leave.*" So, I went to stay overnight the aunt's house to break the isolation feeling. At the time I was 18 years old. When I returned from my visit my sister's husband approached me as soon as I came in the door and accused me of disrespecting his house and told me it would be best if I got my own place and he would pay for it. Not only did that strike me odd but I thought about what's the difference of me staying there and him paying for somewhere else for me to live. Something in my spirit didn't feel right so I called my sister while I was at work and asked her what the issue was; "*Why is your husband telling me that I had to leave and that I disrespected your home when you gave me permission to go spend the weekend away?*" My sister wanted to talk about everything when she got home from work so we ended the call. When my sister got home the conversation resumed and it went left. It was out of the clear blue sky when she said *"Yes – I do think it would be best if you got your own place."* This was a major blow to me! This was not the plan! I arrived in May and was being put out in August.

    I turned to my mother for help and guidance but she had been on assistance her whole life, didn't have any savings and she wasn't in the position to send for me or help me in any way. I had no choice but to find my own place so I got in contact with the cousin that I had given the drugs to and told him the situation. He told me his dad's friend and his son were looking for a roommate. At the time, I didn't know that the friend had recently been released from prison. They only stayed about 30 minutes away from where my sister lived so I decided to stay with them for a while in a two-bedroom apartment. I worked 12 hour shifts at a warehouse job that I had discovered through a temporary agency. The eldest man was around 60 plus years old but he looked like he was 80. We had an arrangement where he would buy all the food and I would pay the rent so it all balanced out to be equal. He told me he done 15 years in prison for killing a man. Despite his past, he and I never had any problems. His son and I however, had a huge problem. He was a 15-year-old boy that would snoop through my things and wear my clothing while I was away working. Weird huh! The main issue became living with this older man him having sex and sneaking around with his best friend's wife. While his best friend would go to work, his wife would come over and drink and have sex with my roommate around the same time every day like it was her job and nobody's business.

After a while, I would get this bad feeling in the pit of my stomach. I knew that one day the best friend would come home and catch them and all hell was going to break loose. All I knew was that I didn't want to be around for that scene. I didn't think I could voice my opinion to them so I called my mom and expressed my concern. I shifted my focus to my next goal. To buy a car so I could get around. I needed a car because of the way Greater Atlanta was set up. The bus didn't come to the suburban area so the only thing left for me to do was move onto a college campus. I had to get away from that situation before it was too late. Every time I moved-- I never looked back. It became a survival mechanism to me and through it all God kept me because I was a sheep amongst the wolves.

I began to pay attention to what was directly in front of me. I never looked to left or to the right. Every time I moved I learned my surroundings to make sure I was by a bus or a train or in walking distance from my job. Through all this I felt that my family didn't care and they didn't even know where I was. Nor did they have that concern of where I might have been. I had faith that God knew what he was doing. He had already shaped and molded me. Despite my upbringing, I realized my mother had taught me how to survive. What I have come to understand and know is that you must keep your eye on the prize, which is God. He will direct your steps. What I know to be true is not everything we go through in life will be easy or comfortable. I have come to the understand that although it might seem bad to someone from the outside looking in, it wasn't that way for me. I felt like something was always going to change and especially when I got my own independence.

    I learned to strive and keep going until I was self-sufficient and safe. It became my unspoken goal. I was thankful God kept me and by His grace and mercy I was never abused. I dated a couple of guys that tried to be physically abusive but that's when my fight mechanism kicked in. I had made up my mind that I would kick, scream and do whatever I had to do to keep me from any hurt, harm or danger. It was going to be them or me and I figured that I had a whole lot of life to live so I was going to fight for it. I later realized that this attitude developed in me due to seeing my oldest sister being abused. I believe that traumatized me. I thought of myself as Winnie Mandela and I said, *"I would not bow down or give up and if you managed to get me down, you'd better make sure that I was out because if I got up that was your tail."*

I had decided that I would not be haunted or be intimidated by the strength of a man. Now that I have grown to be a strong, secure, black woman, I have adjusted many of my ways and learned to have tact, look further than the surface emotions and to make decisions for the betterment of all parties involved. The very thing that was meant to break you is where your strength lies. There will be crossroads in your life. Whichever way you decide to go just know when you think you are at the end of the road you can turn around and go the other direction. Don't stop - keep moving. More times than none that journey will seem lonely but remember you can survive and think of *Footprints in the Sand.*

The Survival Game

Footprints in the Sand – Mary Stevenson

One night I dreamed a dream.
As I was walking along the beach with my Lord.
Across the dark sky flashed scenes from my life.
For each scene, I noticed two sets of footprints in the sand,
One belonging to me and one to my Lord.

After the last scene of my life flashed before me,
I looked back at the footprints in the sand.
I noticed that at many times along the path of my life,
especially at the very lowest and saddest times,
there was only one set of footprints.

This really troubled me, so I asked the Lord about it.
"Lord, you said once I decided to follow you,
You'd walk with me all the way.
But I noticed that during the saddest and most troublesome times of my life, there was only one set of footprints.
I don't understand why, when I needed You the most, You would leave me."

Transition: Ashes Emanating Beauty

He whispered, "My precious child, I love you and will never leave you

Never, ever, during your trials and testings.

When you saw only one set of footprints,

It was then that I carried you."

Shawonia Thomas

Broken Chains

The Bible says, "But they that wait on the Lord shall renew their strength; they shall mount up with wings as eagles; they shall run, and not be weary; they shall walk, and not faint" (Isaiah 40:31). In 2004, I was hospitalized for an emotional breakdown. When I overcame that battle, I vowed to recognize the signs and do whatever I needed to so I would never be in that emotional state again. Things had gotten so bad I gave up on EVERYTHING; life, my kids, work, writing, and even God! What I was going through sucked the life out of me.

Even though I do not recall the exact events and the order of which they occurred, I do remember the day as if it were yesterday. My mind has blocked out some pertinent information from the traumatic event that led up to me being hospitalized but I remember getting in the car. In the hospital, I remember coming to and blacking out again. I was told that I made several phone calls to tell people where I was. Yet, I don't remember calling anyone. I believe I was in shock.

I remember the bright room with the small bed. I remember the nurses standing around me, but I don't remember what they were asking me. I was told by someone on the psychiatric unit of emergency room at Michael Reese Hospital, that I was asked if I felt like hurting myself and my response was "Yes." I know I had to be in a very low place to say that because I would not say anything like that now! Unfortunately, that statement is one of the reasons my hospitalization was initiated. To understand why hospitalization became the outcome, I will take you back to where it all started. As I sit here and write today reflecting on that moment, there is a racing beat in my heart. My breathing flow has changed. And nothing could penetrate my blank stare at this very moment. My mind is switching to an unconscious mode as I begin to dig deep to remember the days leading up to this event.

It was February 2001, the day of my aunt's funeral. After the repass, all my family went back to my mom's place. It was the first time I would meet some of my cousins. We had such a good time; dancing and laughing. I remember one of my cousins was teaching me how to dance; the art of stepping to be exact. I didn't have to pick up the kids that night but I knew I'd better make it home before it got too late, or I was going to hear an ear full of complaining from my, then, fiancé.

Everything that I did seemed to be on a timer. I always had to watch the clock when I was out; checking my watch or my phone, discretely. If I stayed out past a certain time, in his eyes, I was with another man. I lived on the edge of my seat and walked on eggshells. If, all my attention and time was not dedicated to him and meeting his needs, I was worthless and useless. He complained about everything I did outside of the house. He would use his special manipulation tactic. There were always comments about how I didn't care about leaving him in the house by himself, about how the people I was hanging with didn't care about me like he did, and how there was nothing outside for me as a single woman. These comments always made me be more observant of my surroundings, which somehow worked to keep me isolated; isolated from my family; isolated from the world. I became reluctant to go places and if I did, it was only for a moment.

After a while of enjoying my family I decided to head home. I remember I had gotten a rose from the funeral but I left it in the front seat of the car. It had been such a long day; I was so tired, I just wanted to get in the house and go to bed. I had forgotten all about the damn flower, rose, or whatever it was! For whatever reason, he was in my car and when he saw the rose it sent him into a rage. I was in the bed sleeping and all I remember is being awakened by brutal madness! As I was being drug out of bed by my foot, I let out the loudest screams ever.

Transition: Ashes Emanating Beauty

I remember getting kicked and choked. I remember seeing darkness here and there and then seeing some flashes but cannot say what they were. I don't remember how long this went on. I just know it was long enough and one punch too many. Between the blows and the kicks, he was making accusations of me being with another man. His words were, "Do you really think I'm stupid? You just didn't care about me finding the rose, huh?" And then he threw another punch, then another kick, and then more of him blaming me for what he was really doing. *"This is what you wanted! You wanted me to find the rose and get upset"* he said. This was the first of many times of being blamed for his irate and irrational behavior.

Growing up on the South-Side of Chicago, it was understood that when a person wasn't looking and you hit them, it was called a "sucker punch". Who does that? Who sneaks up on someone and gets a lick in? A sucker! I cannot believe I did not call the police that day. It's sad to say that not only did I not make the call, but I froze up and went into a shock. I just laid there, on the floor, balled up in a fetal position, crying my eyes out. They were tears of disbelief and violation. When I finally came back to reality, I moaned and groaned and made my way to the bathroom. In the distance, I could hear him saying, "Baby, I'm sorry.

Broken Chains

Please forgive me! I don't know what came over me!" As I closed the bathroom door, I could hear, "You better not tell anybody!" And that wasn't the only threat. Abusers are manipulative and they use these types of tactics to take control of the situation.

As I soaked in the tub, I thought "How could he do something like that? What did I do to deserve this? What am I going to do?" As I soaked some more, I could vaguely hear footsteps coming towards the door. The knob twisted and I just closed my eyes. He sat on the toilet and began to say what abusers says, *"I'm sorry. I'll never do that again. I didn't mean to do it. I saw the rose and blanked out. I don't want you to leave me. What are you going to do? Please, I can't go to jail."* He left, but a few minutes later, came back and said, *"If you call the police, I swear when I get out I'm gonna kill you!"*

The next day, I laid in bed and cried, treated my wounds, and cried some more. I had to wear long sleeves to cover the bruises on my arms. I found a turtleneck high enough to cover the hand prints and scratches on my neck. My eye was bloodshot red and black. I used my hair to cover it. I asked myself "Why did I go through all of that instead of speaking up? Why did I put myself through that emotional torture?" At that moment, I thought about the threats. At work on Monday, I stayed to myself; very quiet and reserved, keeping my head down so no one would notice my eyes. But somebody did notice. My big sista from the African mother. She took me upstairs to her office and questioned me. The abused know the signs and symptoms of other abused people. She advised me to call the police. Consequently, by the time I got home I could only think about what my fiancé said to me in that bathroom. For that reason alone, I did not make the call. As a result, it gave him the right to strike again; the right to smack me around every time he got mad or blanked out.

He'd use excuses to why he did it, such as - I just smacked you damn! You shouldn't have been talking like that to me, etcetera. Thank God it never happened when my kids were home. After about a year the abuse finally stopped and things got better. We started going to church together and he became the nicest person on the planet earth for a while.

He was a musician; a rapper at his best. He worked on his music and I worked on my writing. I was excited about finally having some peace. I thought we had a breakthrough, a redefined moment in our relationship. He was even talking more about marriage and how he wanted to change. After about five years into our relationship we went to counseling. Even though he was not very open and never admitted his wrong-doings in the abuse, things were turning around. We continued to go to church together and played house for a little while longer (living like a married couple with children). To people looking from the outside, everything probably looked or seemed perfect. I thought if I continued to do what I was doing, giving in to what he wanted, going to church, taking care of the kids and the house, that in the eyes of God, everything else would go away, that all was forgiven and forgotten.

Going to church, school, work and working out at the gym truly opened my eyes to the world. I was reading books on my African heritage, learning new things and becoming a better ME! I was dumping so much knowledge into my mind that it was giving me understanding of who I was; a beautiful, black queen. I was reading books such as *One Day My Soul Just Opened Up,* by Iyanla Vanzant, and *Managing Your Emotions* by Joyce Meyers. All of which gave me insight on how to deal with some of the hurt I had experienced. I enrolled in Kennedy King's Child Development program. School was an escape away from dealing with my hurt and pain. I was having nightmares almost every night. Every so often I would have flashbacks of that very first time. I never truly forgave him but I stayed with him until he died in 2013 and I went to therapy. We got married and even though the abuse wasn't happening anymore, the issues were never resolved, just pushed under the rug. We didn't walk on it but around it. If it wasn't happening we didn't speak about it.

So, I was enrolled in school, working full-time in a Head Start school, and taking care of my body-spiritually and physically. I was learning the difference between healthy and unhealthy, what was damaging, and how to nourish my soul. However, as I was maturing and feeding my mind spiritually, I wasn't fully healing from those traumatic experiences. The longer the hurt was covered the deeper it cut into my soul. It is never good to cover a wound without cleaning it up first, it leaves ugly scars. And one thing you don't want are scabs that won't heal.

The Manipulation

Meanwhile, he was noticing a change in my attitude. I was feeling good; things were calm around the house, I was managing school and taking care of the kids, the housework, work, going to church and still had time to write. I was preparing to get my book published but in reality, I was doing too much. Some nights, staying up until 1 or 2 o'clock in the morning to get things done. He started saying things like, *"How dare you feel good about yourself! You will not look nice and have other men looking at you!"* He began to accuse me of cheating again. But that it is not in my character.

In combination with me being so busy with everything, I had a daughter who was having behavior issues. She was fighting everyone in her class, even the teachers. I was getting phone calls from her school, no one wanted to babysit her, and she was fighting her brothers immensely! She would throw these hour-long tantrums that were unexplainable. It didn't matter where we were, if something was not going her way, she had a meltdown; in the car, in the house, and believe it or not, in stores. My daughter's behavior was uncontrollable. There was so much going on with her during that time it was draining my physical energy. I was taking her to play groups, therapy, doctor's appointments, and trying to figure out the best plan for her. I tried changing her diet, that didn't work. Buying whole foods, counting calories, and keeping track of the sugar intake was expensive and time consuming as well. She had to have an individual schedule and routine for every part of the day, along with a reward system. It truly crushed me when they diagnosed her with being Bipolar.

Transition: Ashes Emanating Beauty

I didn't want to go the medication route because I thought she was too young. I tried changing her sleep patterns and everything that I could think of that would make a difference and change her behavior. I thank God for their grandmother who gave me a break every so often. But during the free moments at home, I spent arguing and fighting the person that was supposed to be there to take some of the burden off me. There is only so much a person can take. During this time of struggle, figuring out what was going on with my daughter, the emotional abuse and manipulation from my fiancé was taking a toll on me.

I was being convinced to isolate myself because *he was the only person that understood me*. I lost friends because I was afraid to hang out for fear that I would be accused of cheating. Sometimes, I would just make excuses when people would invite me places, knowing good and well I didn't have anything else to do. I had to keep track of the time with everything that I did and I became resentful and angry. Eventually, I got fed up and began to fight back. When he threw daggers, I threw them back. When he swung, I swung back. Not only did we fight all over the house, breaking and smashing things, but cleaned up before the kids got home. Then it was back to playing house; cooking, cleaning, helping with homework, and you name whatever else. I picked up the pieces and put on a fake smile for a while. Not to mention, I had to be strong to be able to handle all the business with my daughter.

The Crack That Shattered the Glass

In addition to the breaking, the beating and the fighting, my daughter's behavior had gotten to the most overwhelming stage of her illness. This is when I was learning of what Bipolar was and the symptoms. I was learning my daughter all over again; the Bipolar child. The in-home respite therapy sessions did not work. They just kept her busy while I cooked. She began to tear things up and run away. At this point, her tantrums were so long and drawn out that everyone in the house was being affected. Our nights were spent cleaning up and regrouping from the day. The boys needed so much from me and to be honest, I could not give them one hundred percent.

One day, I had to decide to have her admitted to a hospital. I had to make the call to 9-1-1. That hurt me so bad! No parent wants to see their child hurting, emotionally or physically. My daughter was ill and I knew this was the last option to seeking the help that she needed. We were in the emergency room all night and I believe I didn't make it home until 3 or 4 o'clock in the morning. And oh, there was no calling in from work! With so many of those nights here and there and me going to work with minimum sleep, I was becoming drained, emotionally and physically. I wasn't eating the way I should've been. I wasn't getting enough rest, nor sleep. And I was doing it all by myself. I became so weak in all areas; mind, body, and soul. I allowed the weakness to take over. I was fighting with my flesh and spirit. I was overwhelmed and could not deal with all that was going on any longer; I was crashing! My entire system was shutting down; all but that peace of mind that held on by a thread.

  The fighter in me reached out to the outside world to make them aware of my being. I drove myself to the hospital was a cry out for help. I let go of my faith that was giving me inner strength. I was at the breaking point. Close to having a nervous breakdown. It was a stress overload dealing with my daughter's health issues, school, and worrying about everything in my relationship. My body and mind was feeling like a puzzle with its pieces not in place. But I kept on pushing through. I ignored all the symptoms; a short fuse, fear, panic and anxiety attacks, racing thoughts and crying spells.

  There was not any possibility of reaching out to the family. Growing up with the dominant women in my

Broken Chains

family, it was hard to go to anyone of them and tell them what was going on, especially my mom. My mother respected this man for being with her daughter and helping me raise three children that were not his. Many people called my mom Gangsta Netta-Netta G. She always made it known what she would do to any person, if they did something to me. Besides, I would always think about what it would make ME look like for accepting the malarkey that was going on.

That Day…

I remember having on a white blouse and a black skirt (choir attire), so it must've been a Sunday. We were arguing and of course the kids were not at home. I remember standing in the dining room and getting punched in the nose for talking too loud to him. I went into the kid's room and started praying out loud, talking to God and telling Him, *"I can't take this anymore!"* As I went into a rage, I yelled *"Just kill me now!"* I began to throw things at him and scream. I think I blanked out for a minute because it was still daylight at that time but I only remember being in the car at night; crying profusely, screaming and beating on the steering wheel. We often ask ourselves, *"How did I get here?"* So, let's go back to the beginning of this journey; what led to hospitalization? It wasn't just about what happened THAT day, it was everything that was going on, the constant stress factors, which included, school, my daughter, sleep deprivation, and the toxic relationship. A nervous breakdown is triggered by constant, overwhelming stressors. It's not caused by the everyday life activities, like cooking and cleaning or even something chaotic that happened during a day. I was feeling anxious all the time and it felt like I just broke in half. It was as if I had shattered and nothing could put me back together again. It was worse than Humpty Dumpty's fall! Now I know that it was God who put me back together.

How far did I fall?

As I sat and wrote about these events, I found some notes that I had written from the days that I was in the hospital. One note was from October 24, 2004, at 10:10 am. I was in Michael Reese Psychiatric Unit. And I wrote: I think back to that entire day. I woke up in a rage. It felt as if I was going to explode. I was snapping on everybody about everything. My mind was in a twister state; everything was so mixed up.

It's acceptable to fall but what do you do when you fall? Did you know that you can fall and get back up? Did you know that falling helps to build you up? Sometimes we get so wrapped up in the fall that we lose sight of the opportunity to build up. Your pride is hurt, your feelings are hurt, and the pain can be unbearable. These moments are not meant to allow our lives to drop from under us. We can't allow our struggles to leave us broken. So, broken that the pieces are shattered to the point it's impossible to be put back together. Just know, any glue God uses to fix us will work. In the beginning, I was so weak I could not eat. My spirit was broken but I didn't allow the bottom to fall. I read Psalms 23 over and over:

The Lord is my shepherd; I shall not want. He makes me to lie down in green pastures. He leads me besides the still waters. He restores my soul.

He restores my soul! He restored my soul! He is restoring my soul! I didn't know what else to read. Besides, this was the only thing that was giving me hope. It gave me strength. After reading the passage over and over, it gave me strength to stand! I thought back to all that I was doing leading to my emotional breakdown. I sat on the hospital bed and wrote: Everybody thought I was so strong. I thought I could hold everything together but the truth is, it was just too much. Exactly! I was doing too much. And I should have allowed someone to be there to support me.

Transition: Ashes Emanating Beauty

Tip #1: Stop carrying loads that are bigger than you. There is a God. No, He won't put more on you than you can bear. However, you can know your limit. We don't have to carry our problems on our shoulders or backs. Give it to God! Use your support system; mother, father, friend, sister, brother, cousin, uncle, or even a church member. I didn't talk to anyone about my daughter. I didn't talk to anyone about the abuse. I was being traumatized during one of the most stressful times in my life. Not only was I not releasing the emotional stress of dealing with an ill child and having to send her away for help, I was being violated in every which way; emotionally and physically.

If you are going through a storm and you have people around that are not trying to help you or take some of the weight off your shoulders, they don't need to be in your life! Know who you are. It wasn't until I heard the words, "You are too pretty to be walking around with your face like that", did I start to reflect on the bruises; the black eyes, the scratches, and the fingerprints on my neck and arms from being grabbed and squeezed. Those words came from one of the male workers in the hospital.

I began to read books on healing, emotions, and ways to help yourself with different life struggles. Of course, the doctors prescribed a dosage of a pill or two to keep the other doctors coming. I remember taking Zoloft. It made me cry a lot. I had the trembles, dry mouth, and a loss of appetite. And then at home, he would say *"Make sure you take your medicine because I need you to get better"*. To only find out it was a plot to keep me bound, to have control of me, to break me down even further. This was nothing more than, a manipulation tactic to make me think he really cared. He attempted to make me believe he was concerned about my well-being.

    The put-downs and insulting words that were used to tear me down did not work. "How do you know, you're a psycho! You're weak minded and can't even handle anything". The toxic energy was continuing to drain me but I wouldn't allow it to pull me down. When people you love tell you things about yourself, you tend to believe them because you're thinking, "They love me so they're going to tell me the truth". You take what they say to heart. The truth of the matter is, people can be so manipulating that they feed you a hand full of lies. Professing that they care just to woo you to abuse you even more!

    Tip #2: Get rid of toxic people! Let them go so that you can release the negative energy from your life. Toxic people instill toxic messages into the people that love them. If someone that loves you tells you that something is wrong with you, beware of how and when they tell you. Yes, you're going to value what they say but make sure it's a heartfelt comment or suggestion.

The Build-Up

Once I started reading my bible more, going to church consistently, reading different books to enhance my knowledge, and doing things to build my self-esteem, I began to find peace again. It also triggered some things with the man (my fiancé). This time, I ignored his behavior and focused on ME. I used my spirituality as my weapon. I began to find ME. I also read books about my sexuality; being a woman and what came along with that meaning.

I had many visits to the local library during this time. I checked out books on my African heritage and culture. I listened to gospel music around the clock (and still do). Yolanda Adams kept telling me that the battle was not mine. Through the pain I was inspired to write again. During these days, I wrote some of my best poems; with a focus on being an inspiration to others. You know they say, "When you minister to others you minister to yourself". I would spend hours writing. Sometimes I would sit on the porch, at my desk, or the living room floor, sipping my wine and dive in. The pen would hit the paper and that would be all she wrote. I would find passages in the bible that would relate to what I was going through or what I was feeling. This helped me to appreciate life more; looking at my dreams and goals, and thanking my creator for making me who I am.

Tip #3: Find YOU and your spirituality: Find your YOU. Who are you? What is your purpose? Where are you going? What do you want to do? Get to know who you are by spending time with yourself. Have some quiet, alone time with YOU! Get to know your spiritual side and the purpose you have been purposed to live. Get connected to the deeper part of life, the reason why you are living.

My knowledge and understanding of my spirituality helped me to fight against mental destruction. I started writing my feelings in a journal that I used as an outlet. It helped me to relax and tap into the side of me that's hidden from the outside world. Once I let the pen touch the paper, I released it all. It is so very important to have a way to release negative energy; it's something about releasing words onto paper. After writing, my mind would be set free of the stress around me. It was then that my dream came to light. The inspirational poems gave me an idea to have my own greeting card line. One of these days it will be manifested.

Tip #4: Find a Hobby: If you don't have a hobby, think about something you like doing in your spare time and be more consistent with it. If you find joy in it, it can become your hobby; painting, sculpting, knitting, writing, or even a sport. A special skill or talent that you never knew you had.

Yes, writing helped me tremendously in releasing the strain on my brain. The most effective approach that I took in the "build-up" process was being true to myself; listening to that inner voice that was telling me not to accept the garbage anymore. One of my favorite quotes is:

God, grant me the serenity to accept the things I cannot change, change the things I can, and wisdom to know the difference!

More importantly, I began to fight back with the power that God gave me. I prayed and fasted, during which I sought guidance for how to overcome the barriers that were interfering with my true happiness. I focused more on taking care of ME; doing ME, protecting ME, and being ME!

Broken Chains

Rick Warren wrote a book called, *The Purpose Driven Life; What on Earth Am I Here For?* In the hope that I would see some changes in my life, I decided to read this book. I am glad I took the 40-day spiritual journey that gave me a deeper insight on why I was created. I fell in-love with God, my creator. And began loving myself all over again. And still today I am believing that I am "not an accident". Just when life was seaming so meaningless with everything that was going on, I began to feel as though there was hope. I began to do some true soul-searching and make life-changing decisions that created a dramatic transformation; my transition to better!

One of the strategies that was suggested in the healing journey was to make sure I was communicating my feelings. The bible says, "If your brother sins against you, go and tell him his fault" (Matthew 18:15). Once you've shared your hurt to the person who betrayed you, the next step is to give that person a chance to acknowledge your feelings. And I did just that; I shared my feelings about the drama and how I wanted a change. Naturally, people apologize and change their behavior, discontinue the hurt that they cause, and try to do better. Not in this case; I was blamed for everything that was going on and all I could give back was a disappointing look.

Transition: Ashes Emanating Beauty

It was time for a serious change. I had to make a decision that would affect everyone, especially my children. During this time, I was looking for a house to purchase. It was either stay and deal with the madness until I found something, or pick up and start over. I chose to get out! I put everything in storage and went and stayed with a relative. I sacrificed my comfort to have my peace of mind, my sanity. Even though I was using all the different strategies mentioned, the toxic energy was pulling at me and I couldn't take it anymore; so, I left. I had doubt at first; that I could even do it on my own, but I had to keep the faith. For six months, I shared a bedroom with my children, and although they would ask, "Where's (the man)", my peace of mind was their road to healthiness.

Sometimes we fail to realize that our mental stability has a strong effect on our children. They know when something's not right; they know when mommy is sad. Mommy was broken on the inside and needed some time to herself, to be fixed. Leaving was one of the hardest things I ever had to do, but I was free! I freed myself from something that could've taken me back down and I refused to go down again. It was unhealthy and unsafe for me and my children. I could not be the best mom I could be if I had stayed. Even though the physical contact seized, the emotional abuse was just as torturous. I was becoming numb and it was suffocating me.

I continued to go to church, joining the choir and doing other ministry work. I got the boys involved as well and kept them busy. We had frequent visits with my daughter, I made sure of that; we just made it family time every other week. I accepted what God was doing with her and me. She was being well taken care of at the facility she was placed in and it was allowing me to breathe and focus on the boys. I continued to read and write in my spare time. And most importantly, I could laugh again!

Lessons Learned

I learned to not carry so much on my plate and allow those around to help me. I used to be so prideful and not include others in "the help." I was so used to doing it all but I had to learn how to involve people in my system; to allow people to do things FOR me. I also had to involve God! Sometimes, we forget to pray and ask God for help when we need Him the most.

Another source I used was a recovery program. This program was for individuals who needed some type of healing. We met at a church, participated in worship service, and went into our groups. The group I was placed in was filled with women who were experiencing a loss or going through a phase of being controlled by their husbands. In the beginning, I did not speak much, just listened. After a few weeks, I began to open up and answer a few questions and even gave a little feedback and suggestions to the other women. I remembered the title of one of the books I had read, *One Day My Soul Just Opened.* It's okay to seek help and allow others to walk with you through your healing process. I had to learn that it was perfectly normal to seek help. I felt so relieved when I completed the program.

If you find yourself carrying a load that's bigger than you, STOP and unload. The first step is to give it to God. Next, use your support system and find someone you can trust that can help you through your struggles. Don't be too private where no one knows what's going on in your life. You don't have to tell all your business but there needs to be at least one person you can confide in. Holding things inside like I did can cause great damage to your nervous system, which is why I had a nervous breakdown!

If you feel like an emotional wreck...

If you feel tired and exhausted...

If you feel like giving up...

Broken Chains

You are probably suffering from physical or mental exhaustion. Know the signs before it is too late. Find an outlet and get help. Figure out the cause of your breakdown and come up with strategies of how to deal with it. There is a build-up process that can happen before the breakdown, before the fall. And if you've already fallen, you CAN get back up!

It is with my deepest sympathy to share that the man who abused me, is no longer living. I have finally healed from the hurt and pain, and moved on with living the life that God purposed for me. I am now happily married to my soulmate. My husband was placed in my life during my time of bereavement and he was the first person I told my story to. I can honestly say that it is so much easier to get over obstacles because of the strategies I used to deal with stress. I have a strong support system and my faith in God helps me believe that I can give Him my problems. And above all else, Prayer Works!

It's a terrible shame
That we must go through the ups and downs of life.
It's a shame that the crisis
Of one too many falls can be the blame
Of why we can't get back up.

Transition: Ashes Emanating Beauty

We fail to realize

That it's not the fall

But the build-up

That makes us stronger.

It's not the fall

But the process

That makes us a survivor.

It's the in-between of the meantime

Of the journey of reality

Of accepting the possibilities

Of our lives falling beneath our feet.

What do we do?

We get back up.

And we fight for what we believe;

Believe that there is a God, who will mend you,

Who will fix you! Who can make you feel brand new!

Evelyn R. Donelson, M. E

Transition: Ashes Emanating Beauty

"In any situation, you can choose to be bitter or better." – Anonymous

Can you imagine going through life feeling less than a human being? You have the gnawing feeling in the pit of your belly that God created you to be something great but you do not feel worthy of it? Being ashamed of who you are, feeling rejected by every relationship, and no matter how hard you try, it seems to never be enough for anyone in your life. For most my life, this is how I felt. I went from relationship to relationship trying to be enough of a woman to receive the love I desperately desired, just wanting someone to love me for who I am and not for what I could give them. It wasn't until I hit rock bottom did I finally get the revelation that I have always been enough for God!

At 19, I became a mother, stepmother and then a wife. I had never addressed the emotional, physical and sexual abuse issues of my childhood. I carried all my baggage into the marriage and so did my spouse. We were two broken kids now married with children and we struggled financially, emotionally, and spiritually. Regardless of what happened, I would not leave. The marriage was filled with many forms of abuse: alcohol, drugs, verbal and emotional. But it was never physical until the final day.

    It was the summer of 1992. I had been at our local teen hangout as usual and as I was leaving, I heard, "Excuse me, can I go with you?" I turned around, smiled and gave a side eye glance before reluctantly responding, "Probably not!" He laughed and so did I. Little did I know we were going to the same destination. The Hammer Droppers; an after-hours club. There, he found me and struck up a conversation before we exchanged numbers. After that night, we talked on the phone for hours at a time. Almost instantly, our relationship became sexual in nature. He was handsome, attentive, charming and was in the street life - deep. My type of guy. All I could think of was, out of all the women he could have chosen; he chose me. I felt extremely special for the first time in my life. We dated off and on for two years prior to moving in together and creating a family with dynamics neither of us understood. Creating and continuing generational cycles of abuse, brokenness and poverty.

    Finally, I had the one thing I always wanted: someone to love me for me. He loved me, flaws and all. We shared all the secrets of our lives with each other vowing to be together forever. I was his queen and he was my king. After five years and two more children, we decided it was time to become official; we got married. I was in fairytale heaven, refusing to believe my life was really a mess. Then it happened and I was devastated. One year after saying, "I do, forever", I realized he had been cheating. I had heard it for years but I just didn't see it or want to believe it. *He wouldn't do that to me*, I thought. We had grown together and no one could break our bond, or so I thought. But, oh to my surprise, I was about to get a rude awakening.

In December 2003, I was certain I wanted to know for myself if he was and had been cheating. I told myself on January 1, 2004 I would start my own investigation, so I purchased a purse calendar and started the tracking. Every move that he made I wrote in the calendar; whether good or bad days, I wrote them down. I wanted and needed to know. I had to track the his every move. It was up to me to find out what was going on and if I have been a fool all this time. Not only did I track his pattern, I started to research the phone bills. I knew something was going on but I just couldn't put my finger on it. After eight months, I had the evidence that I needed. I had obtained the other woman's phone number from our phone bills. One day after work I decided to confront him, asking if he had his cell phone.

Pain to Purpose

"Mine is dead," I said. "I need to use your phone really quick." He pulled out his phone and waited. "Dial this number." As I gave him the number, he stopped dialing midstream. He couldn't believe that I had the phone number. "Why did you stop? Dial the number," I told him. He asked, "Why do you want me to call this number?" I responded, "Why not, you call it all times of the day while you're at work. You call her more than you talk to me during the day," As we sat there, I contemplated what should happen next. He looked nervous, so I finally responded, "You know what, it doesn't even matter anymore." At that very moment, I decided it was over.

From that hot day in August of 2004 until May 2005 I was in a total depression. I'm not even sure how my children were cared for, got to school or even ate. I checked out of life because I just could not believe that this had happened. During the depression, I had often thought of killing everyone in the home. I had even planned it so I knew exactly how I would do it. I would use our double barrel 12-gauge shotgun, killing the kids first and then him and finally myself. One day, life had become too much to bare. I sat in the car and cried and cried. I could not stop crying; it was uncontrollable. My friend stopped by my house and she saw me sitting in the car so she got in and

Transition: Ashes Emanating Beauty

asked me what was wrong. I wouldn't tell her. I continued to cry and she just sat there with me. After a while she began to pray. Then she started singing. She has a beautiful voice. We sat in the car for hours with me crying and her alternating between praying and singing. Finally, I started to open up and tell her my thoughts of killing everyone in our home so that my pain would stop. I rationalized that by killing the children, no one would have to worry about taking care of them. She began to tell me how God would not want that and it's the trick of the enemy because I had a calling on my life. I began to cry again and I remember saying, "I just can't take this anymore. I'm tired." She began to pray again. This time I felt different. I dried the tears on my face as she continued to give me scripture references and telling me how God had something for me to do. Although I couldn't see it, she knew it was there. I shared with her how I caught him cheating and she assured me that God would see me through. At that time, I was a believer but I wasn't saved nor was I trying to serve God.

By the grace of God and because of His obedient angel, I decided to give our lives one more chance. I began attending church with my friend and on October 5, 2005, I was saved. I started living my life for Christ but the call for drugs and alcohol was overwhelming and I backslid. I stayed with my ex-husband for three more years.

On August 8, 2008, I had enough. He had stayed out all night, again! I barricaded the doors so when he came home he could not get in. As the day went on, my sister convinced me to go with her to the State Fair. I had to get dressed so she took the children (mine and hers) to McDonald's, so I thought. As I was getting dressed, I heard someone come in the house. I thought it was my sister, but he kicked in our bedroom door and I could see death in this eyes. He started choking me, pinning me against the wall. I could feel myself getting light headed, so I scanned the room for a weapon and noticed a steel bat behind the bedroom door. I had to get to it or I was going to die. I began to fight for my life. I got him off me and ran towards the door, grabbing the bat as I darted up the steps to get away. This was the first time he ever put his hands on me. I was in shock. For some reason, I didn't run out of the house. All I could think was, *I'm not going out without a fight*. He ran after me and when he got to the top of the steps, I hit him with the bat. By now, my sister had run into the house and saw me at the top of the stairs. She instantly grabbed a weapon. After he realized I was going to fight, he went back downstairs and got his gun. The back door was still barricaded and I had to pass him to get out the front. As he came up the steps, he dropped the bullets to the gun. My heart was racing and my sister was screaming. It was like he didn't even see her. His jet-black eyes were fixed on me. When he got to the last step I knew I was about to die. I grabbed his hand with the gun in it and we began to tussle. I could hear my sister yelling at the 911 dispatcher, "My brother-in-law is trying to kill my sister; he's going to shoot her, please help." Somehow, he twisted my hand with his and put the loaded gun to my chest before pulling the trigger. The gun jammed, and I remember thinking, *My kids can't find me like this*. That's when I felt the supernatural strength. I overpowered him, pouncing on top of him like a lion, with one knee in his throat and the other on his arm with the hand that held the gun. I screamed, "What is wrong with you, why are you doing this?" It was like a light clicked on in his head. He jumped up, tossing me across the room, and ran out the front door. By the grace of God, I'm still here.

That very day, I left and never looked back. Once again, after seven years I was in a space I did not want to be. Alone and loveless. I didn't know what to do. This was the first time we had been apart since we were 19. I knew that I couldn't go back. And I needed to keep me and my children safe. But all of me longed to go back to my comfortable space. For the first time ever, I knew that I had a calling on my life but I didn't know how to get out of the mess I had created. I began to seek God regularly. By this time, I was off drugs completely but I was still drinking. I would go to work, come home, drink and talk to God. For three years, He pruned me, taking me through all of my hurt and pain. He began to show me that the only way out was through Him. I began to lean on the Lord more than I had ever done before and my evolution was underway.

Although I was saved in 2005 I was not fully committed to God until January 1, 2012. Amid my contentment, something I never thought would happen again actually happened; I fell in love. This time I thought it was different. I believed he was Heaven sent and my second marriage would last forever. We dated for a few years prior to planning the wedding. He was everything I had asked for: loving, *honest*, romantic, independent, and he loved my children (who didn't meet him for the first two years) as well as treating me like a queen. We went to church together, prayed together, planned our every move together; we were best friends. We got married and it was supposed to be happily ever after. Almost instantly after exchanging vows, rings and saying, "I Do", he changed.

Transition: Ashes Emanating Beauty

We didn't do anything together anymore. I was totally blindsided, having no idea it had all been an act. There was no more pampering, no more cooking, no more loving the Lord, nor sharing responsibilities. Everything stopped. I began to see that I married Dr. Jekyll and Mr. Hyde. A few months into the marriage, I discovered he divorced his ex-wife six months prior to us being married. Hindsight is 20/20, yet I am sure there were signs I missed or ignored but I just can't recall them because I was so happy.

During my prayer time, I said, "Lord how could this happen again? I just knew that You sent him! I wanted this to last forever!" But God was silent. Because I didn't want to seem like a failure, I tried to stick it out. Once again, I was crushed on the inside. I didn't understand it then but it is in the crushing that the anointing flows. It was during this time God gave me three interactive workbooks titled, *The Process of Change*. I did not know at the time that this was my second chance to a new beginning.

The books were only the start of everything. I had finally gotten the stories out of my system; I was free and able to begin to live. I could see clearly and was able to move forward. As I continued to struggle through the second failing marriage, I founded Power-N-You™, a personal development coaching enterprise. I poured myself into the business all day and night, learning all I could. I did everything possible to keep from coming to the realization that I was facing another divorce.

On November 16, 2014, I decided to call it quits. We had just had a heated discussion and he punched a hole into the door. Immediately, I recognized the signs. The violence. The flashback. It was OVER! It had only been a short eight months that we were married before we went through the divorce and I just didn't understand. During my prayer time one day, I asked God, "Lord did I hear you wrong? Did You tell me not to do this? Was I only supposed to be learning a lesson and I got confused? If so, please forgive me and let's move on." I accepted my truth. I hadn't waited on God nor did I seek Him before moving forward with the marriage. The glitter was there but there was no gold. Although I was crushed, I didn't fall into a depression and I knew God was still there. I was so excited. I passed my test! I learned two valuable lessons. Although I made a mistake, I didn't lose contact with God and I learned I could love again.

Through it all, I continued to go to church and worship God. But there became a pull that I just couldn't explain. So, I began to pray and ask God, *"What is it that I'm supposed to be doing?"* and, *"Why do I feel this way?"*

Transition: Ashes Emanating Beauty

And, He began to unfold the best parts of my new life right in front of my eyes. I shared a piece of my testimony at church one day and after service I was asked to speak at an event. I was so nervous at my first speaking engagement that my knees were shaking, my voice was cracking, and I just could not believe that God had called such a mess to share with so many people. The room was packed and women were staring at me just to hear what I had to say. As I began to speak, I kept thinking, *Why me?* I was asking God "How am I supposed to do this, they're going to think I'm crazy!" I started to tell my story and people began crying, people were praising God and others were shouting. God showed me that day how my pain was turned into my purpose. It was all happening right in front of me. After I spoke, people were coming up to me saying, "*I didn't know that you went through all that! You don't look like what you've been through,*" and, "*Thank you for sharing your testimony because it helped me.*" I praised God on a great scale from that day on.

    I had no idea that my life would never be the same. It was one engagement after another continually for months. God began to put people in my life that knew the speaking and coaching business. I was speaking more, had written the books, and now I was able to begin firmly establishing the coaching enterprise. Although I had been helping women through difficult relationship issues ever since my divorce, I had no idea coaching was something I could get paid to do. Almost immediately, I gained several clients and sold a couple hundred workbooks. I couldn't believe it. I was finally feeling fulfilled. I was being used by God and knew without a doubt He loved me, no matter what. I was finally on track. And I believed God was pleased.

Out of all the adversity I have overcome in my life, I would have never believed God would use me the way that He has. I am clear on what my purpose is and I walk confidently in my God given power. I am determined to help as many women (men when the time calls for it) as God sees fit. With the programs that He has given me, I will be able to assist women with shifting their mindsets so that they too can accept their purpose and walk in their God given power!

This story is only a piece of the tip of my iceberg. Going through these situations allowed me to learn several things about God, myself and others. I pray my lessons help you in this journey of life. It is important that you:

Transition: Ashes Emanating Beauty

- ➢ Be honest with yourself, own your decisions and do not easily dismiss the warning signs in relationships.
- ➢ Know that nothing you have been through will be wasted. It will all be used for the Glory of God. So, I encourage you to stay the course.
- ➢ Seek God in all you do, stay focused on God no matter what it looks or feels like and stay sober minded in the spirit and natural realms.

Going through the situations in my previous marriages demanded I grow emotionally, mentally and spiritually. I would not have conceived this journey in my worst dream. But, without it, I would not be able to help those I am called to help. I thank God for every trial, tribulation and setback because it not only showed me the POWER within but it also taught me I can truly trust God in all things and the POWER of His might. So, do not despise the pain you go through.

Meet the Authors

Meet the Authors of Transition: Ashes Emanating Beauty

Meet the Authors

Precious S. Brown is a Michigan native and dedicated to uplifting the community. She graduated from Indiana Wesleyan University in 2004. She is a sought-after speaker and transition coach. She works tirelessly to bring inspiration and motivation to those who are looking to improve their lives.

Precious is a certified life coach and writing expert. She is the Founder of Pen A Masterpiece, LLC & Kilgore Publishing, LLC where she has written and released her interactive workbook series *The Process of Change*, the best-selling book *Transition: Create the Life You Desire* and *Transition: Ashes Emanating Beauty*. She currently assists aspiring women authors create masterpieces by writing their story and sharing their journey through the power of the pen. Allowing them to shift pain to power, becoming their best selves and establishing their voices in the marketplace.

Precious has facilitated and participated in live and virtual workshops, conferences, and summits across the globe all with the focus of activating the word power lying dormant in the lives of women. She has been helping women for over nine years and knows that it is her God given purpose.

Meet the Authors

For booking events, coaching or speaking engagements, please visit her website www.penamasterpiece.com or email info@penamasterpiece.com.

You are welcomed and encouraged to connect with Precious on Social Media using these links:

Facebook: www.facebook.com/justpreciousb

Instagram: www.instagram.com/justpreciousb

Twitter: www.twitter.com/justpreciousb

Periscope: www.periscope.tv/justpreciousb

Meet the Authors

Tyree L. Groves is a single mother of 2 wonderful sons Louis Emmanuel (22) and Kyle Alexander (17) Groves, youngest sister to Jackie Dixon and Leslee Washington, and daughter to Louis and Martha Groves.

She has always had a genuine passion for customer service and feels currently, it is a dying art form. She was raised in a mom and pop grocery store and being raise by sanctified parents in the south, it had a way of making it easy for you to be a respectful, accountable and a well-rounded great employee.

Tyree currently lives in the small town of Drew, MS. She is an administrative assistant for Mental Health with MHM working on the grounds Mississippi Department of Corrections for the last 5 years. She has enjoyed working in some type of office setting for the last 20 years. She began her carrier in the field as a cold caller (telemarketer) for a carpet cleaning service. This didn't go very well; however, it did help her find her voice. It is amazing that the sound of your voice will determine your success in this type of field.

Tyree is and aspiring entrepreneur and is eagerly anticipating the life changing opportunities that she is destined to achieve.

Meet the Authors

Valencia Griffin-Wallace is a Bestselling author, Valencia Griffin-Wallace has earned the title the southern belle of BOLD, Brave Optimistic Life by Design. CEO and founder of several businesses including Life by Design, she learned that nothing was out of her reach. Growing up, she faced low self-esteem, abandonment, and many other things that kept her on survival mode. Through her trials she created a BOLD mindset, which changed the course of her life. Now as a mentor, she teaches women how to get release the autopilot mindset and design the life they deserve to live.

Valencia's no-nonsense style has earned her many titles. She is a sought-after speaker with her focus on mindset, transformation, and strategy. As the creator and host of Healing U, Define U Radio, DYS-Define Yourself Series, and Define U Movement, she created platforms to educate, enlighten, and empower audiences in life, money, and business.

Valencia is one of the co-authors of the best-selling book ***Transition: Create the Life You Desire***, the author of ***31 Days to Building Your BOLD Factor***, and ***Life Required***. In her downtime, she enjoys being a contributing writer for SWAGHER magazine.

Meet the Authors

"Going through any and everything gives you a certain strength, courage, and wisdom in life. Once you live and learn the lesson, it is your responsibility to teach others the HOW!" -Valencia Griffin-Wallace

To connect with Valencia you can go to her website:

http://www.valenciagwallace.com

Facebook: https://www.facebook.com/valenciagw/

LinkedIN: https://www.linkedin.com/in/valenciagwallace

Meet the Authors

Tasheikya Hunter is a Flint MI native. As a teenage mother, she had many barriers and obstacles to overcome. She succumbed to promiscuity, domestic violence and even homelessness. She began to regain control of her life in 2005 when she graduated from Baker College with a certificate in Medical Billing and Coding. She is currently on the Advisory Board for the college. She is the Credentialing Specialist at Hamilton Community Health Network.

Tasheikya has a passion for helping others; especially the youth, Kingdom building, praise dancing and Evangelism. She had a major spiritual growth spurt while on an Evangelism trip in the Caribbean Island in 2015. Upon returning she was inspired to manifest her vision for a personal model called D.E.P.T.H which means determination, endurance, perseverance, truth, and happiness. She has created opportunities for herself to serve in various capacities such as previously owning a 24-hour daycare center and now heads a dance ministry called Young Ladies Walking for Christ.

Tasheikya is very artistic and creative. Which led her to start her own event planning and costume designs company - M'Kaddesh Designs. She is the founder of G.O.A.L.S (Gaining Outstanding Achievements while

Meet the Authors

Living successfully), and Coordinates yearly community picnics. As a survivor of harsh circumstances Tasheikya has proven to be resilient. She has renewed her life and faith. She is married to Milando Hunter and they have 5 children and one grandchild.

You can connect with Tasheikya by emailing her mahunter77@gmail.com or on any of the social media platforms listed below:

Twitter: www.twitter.com/marchellahunter
Facebook: www.facebook.com/tasheikyahunter
Instagram: www.instagram.com/ladychella77

Meet the Authors

Shawonia D. Thomas is a Flint, Michigan

native who resides in Dallas, Georgia. She is a Master Cosmetologist, an entrepreneur, mentor, teacher and mother of 2 beautiful children. She is currently pursuing a Business Management degree at American InterContinental University and focusing on creating a legacy for her children while sharing her process along the way.

Shawonia is passionate about healing, mentoring teenage girls, giving and growth. She shares her gift and purpose through mentoring. After her experience with the organization, 4girls Inc., where she sponsored a nine-member family for Christmas, she was inspired to become the Visionary and Founder of Jabez Girls Society, Inc. Survivorship is her story.

She is a flower plucked out of the garden placed in a beautiful vase. Her core principles are live and let live, Let your best self shine & keep your head up! One of her greatest accomplishments as a professional is being a civil federal employee for the past 15 years and being a lead investigative technician. Her application to resolve situations and tasks with simplicity and empathy has allowed her to elevate professionally and become the conduit for persons of her agency.

Meet the Authors

Shawonia hopes to share her story and apply all her beauty and health skills, that she has acquired, to the Jabez Girls. She is committed to empowering everyone that crosses her path. You are welcome to connect with Shawonia by visiting her website www.totallifechanges.com or on any of the below social media platforms:

LinkedIN: www.linkedin.com/in/thomas-shawonia-32948657

Facebook: www.facebook.com/shawoniathomas

Facebook Group: @Lipnotic by Shawonia

Meet the Authors

𝐸𝑣𝑒𝑙𝑦𝑛 𝐷𝑜𝑛𝑒𝑙𝑠𝑜𝑛 is a Chicago, Illinois native who is dedicated to education. She is a graduate of National-Louis University where she obtained her Bachelor's Degree in Early Childhood Education, with a minor in Psychology. She has also obtained her Master's in Education with a focus in Special Education and a Certificate in Autism from Kansas University online program. Her desire is to build her Education Consulting Business which led her to pursue a Master's degree in Organizational Management with a Specialization in Leadership from Ashford University.

Her first love is working with children and families which led her to her current position as Special Education Teacher. She is the recipient of the Outstanding Educator Award from the Congressman's Office of Danny Davis in Chicago, Illinois.

Evelyn currently uses her knowledge and experience within her church's leadership ministry. She loves to sing in the choir and write in her spare time. She has been writing poetry since she was a teenager with the goal of having her work formerly published so that her words may inspire women who share similar life struggles as she has. She desires to launch and Inspirational Card Line in the years to come. She believes that her story will

Meet the Authors

help others overcome barriers that may keep them from fulfilling their purpose. You are can contact Evelyn via email Edonelson35@gmail.com or inspirationalpsalms@gmail.com and be sure to her Facebook business page:

https://www.facebook.com/Inspirational-Psalms-4-U-1869377950012063/

www.ingramcontent.com/pod-product-compliance
Lightning Source LLC
Chambersburg PA
CBHW060610100426
42744CB00008B/1382